DRAMATIC HERITAGE

Paul Green

DRAMATIC
HERITAGE

Samuel French

NEW YORK   HOLLYWOOD

SAMUEL FRENCH Ltd.   London

N.C.
814
G

DAVID STEVENS

who has done so much for the American people's theatre.

Several of these essays have appeared in The New York *Times, Theatre Arts, The Bulletin* of the National Theatre Conference, *Tomorrow, College English,* and as syndicated articles in a number of Japanese and American newspapers. I gratefully acknowledge permission to reprint them here in revised form. Also thanks are due the University of North Carolina Press for the use of some material from my former volume *The Hawthorn Tree.*

"The swans go on up the path of the sun,
  They go through the bright air on their miraculous wings."

Contents

DRAMATIC HERITAGE

The Folk Arts

The folk arts are the soul and inspiration of a people's life, and as they thrive so do the people thrive—thrive imaginatively and spiritually.

Br'er Rabbit is worth a dozen millionaires in the well-being of the Republic. And Jack-muh-Lantern himself is beyond price.

Put a question to that old hoary folk character Paul Bunyan who dug out the Great Lakes the year the blue snow fell and turned into ink, and who combed his beard with a scraggly pine tree while he lay resting in the sun.

Or make speech with that great fighter Davy Crockett who swallowed a thunderbolt from heaven—that time he had his mouth open making a political speech in a thunderstorm. And the thunderbolt never hurt him—soured his stomach a bit, but that was all. And later he went home with a piece of the sunrise in his pocket. That's the way I heard it.

Or walk way out wide and handsome and consult with John Henry the Negro muscle-man who led the last showdown fight between the tool and the machine and lost his life in the battle but who now lives on in the minds of every lover of Negro folklore.

"What's that noise we hear, Mammy, like timber crackling yonder?"

"That's John Henry's hammer, chillun, John Henry's nine-pound hammer falling in the sky."

Or go have talk with Mike Fink the fighter, or Stackolee the bad man, or Roy Bean, or Buffalo Bill, or Casey Jones, or gentle and earth-blessing Johnny Appleseed, or the Arkansas Traveler, or even that same prideful prancing Br'er Rabbit.

Or make a query of red-headed Thomas Jefferson where he watches on Monticello Hill, or of George Washington muffled and eternal behind his Mt. Vernon ivied tomb, or the image of Lincoln marbled and profound and guarded beneath his columns there on Potomac River.

They all speak up with one affirming voice of creation and work, denying all weakness and chances gone among us. They proclaim that this nation is a mighty people and up to thundering and mighty things, collectively and individually, and we must take care that this be our continued glory, our burden and our song.

Geographically, industrially, meteorologically, sociologically, we are one of the most active, yeasty and upheaving regions of the earth. And vastness, power and daring reach are our middle name.

II

Once in a burned-out region of Tennessee, amid sulphur fumes, smoking slag heaps and desolation, I saw a native leaning against his cabin door, playing his mouth-organ and watching the evening sun go down. And the scene around him was illumined in a kind of hellish glory. He shook his head at it all and said to me, "I jest couldn't feel at home anywhere else, it's so purty here." And beautiful it was to him and that in spite of the fact that a WPA welfare worker was at the moment trying to persuade him to learn to wear shoes and go to the movies to see Lana Turner—in order that his soul might be lifted up and his social betterment assured.

In passing I plead that this native son be allowed to stay where he is, unhelped by sprout of grass or bird or living tree though he be, yet even so with his mouth-organ finding his life of beauty-in-ugliness sufficient to the day thereof.

A genial and mystic poet from Ireland once told me he found our country too huge and raw and dynamic and un-humanized for his comfort and praise. He couldn't feel close and warm to it, couldn't take it to his bosom's love and appreciation the way he could the little byways, bogs, and lanes of Ireland. And beauty is only to be found, he said, where one can cherish the object, feel and know the sources and tokens of beauty, can endow them or depict them with his own imagination, can know and sense them closely and intimately. One square mile of Irish soil he found preeminently beautiful and loved it in accordance with its beauty. And why not? "For," said he, "I've painted every square yard of it there in Ireland." The distances here he found too great, with too much wild and uprooted life and piled stumps and entrails of earth showing, too much of time's riches going to waste—from the thundering and fire-bitten forests of the northwest to the vast gut of New York City spewing its sewage and human refuse into the cavernous depths of the Atlantic Ocean.

He found the American citizens rushing hither and yon over these vast distances between two oceans, he said, harnessing and conquering and building and trading—whether in turbines, soap, leather, gew-gaws, hairpins, jewsharps, or chewing gum. And always the challenge was to shape, to fashion, to create—always a too keen and overflooding challenge, he said. Here were rivers still to be dredged, jetties to be made, and ever the viaducts and cables reaching, and bridges and mighty cranes lifting and gouging and dumping their load, as man harnessed nature and her things to his will and purpose.

One morning this poet awoke in New Orleans, he recounted, and looking out of his window gazed upon the flat fog-shrouded Mississippi. What an uncouth, wild, and barbaric name after all! And suitable. And showing up like black primeval fish seeking air, the grimy wet snag of stumps and trees protruded menacingly through the fog. A nightmarish and maleficent nature unloosed! And it oppressed him to think that the river stretched far away through limitless mud and prairie grass to the Great Lakes to the north, lying huge and uncouth like a weighty mud-colored serpent across a continent.

And everywhere power, strength, spilling richness and ugliness. And there was no time for meditation, he said.

III

True, we have too often lost the urge and sweetness of meditation, the contemplative process in the practical splurge of doing things—of trading and barter, of being busy and creating a pother of theories, new-fangled creeds and things, when more thoughtfulness and less frenzy would have been better by every test. But we are a pioneer, a building creative nation mainly, delighting in enormous turnovers of goods, services, and ever new enterprises, and immediacy is sometimes overpowering.

And even so the joy, the delight, the emotions of this creativeness we have celebrated in our arts. In our folk arts we have and in our sophisticated ones we shall.

For here to our hand, with the possible leisure which ever more and more perfect servant machines are providing for us, is the chance to create a culture, a joyous way of living, a vibrant idealism, the like of which has occurred perhaps only a few times in the history of the world.

For it is mainly by the glory of its thoughts, its ideals, its imagination that a nation or an age is finally great.

And we are beginning to work hard for that.

Our schools are taking up our native American music—our ballads, folk-songs, work-songs, folk-hymns. More and more our young composers are using the lyrical material of our fields, and hills, and mines, and factories, and halls. Our dramatists are going to the basic and active imaginative life of the people for their subject matter. They are discovering America and her riches for themselves. And the same is true of our poets, painters and crafters. They are all discovering—and in discovering, helping along the process of creativeness—discovering the essential folk-life of the people. And some-day soon the green-growing joy of our dreams and our arts will be set up in the full sunlight of economic favor.

And it is high time already.

For now the frontier is over for us—the spatial, horizontal frontier in which we formerly were wont to extend our rest-less personalities. The last golden yard of California has been explored—we have come to a definite sense of our neighbors, south and north and of the oceans on either side, and of the round, round globe.

Ahead in time, not space, is our period of intensification—of a smelting, of a processing, and distributing the stuff of our nation—of learning to know and express ourselves from within and not by the dull and witless aping of authority, of ill-conceived and second-hand commentaries. And that means first of all that we should know and appreciate our tradition, our past, our folk-arts. And knowing them, appreciating them, means using them in a vital creative way—the way of art.

IV

That's what I mean too—life as an art:—green winter fields even to the lyric, lazy, and indulgent South; paint on the houses, flowers at the door, and care and beauty and love surrounding our bare, pitiful little country schools and churches. Lights and water and conveniences for men and their housewives, not that they may snooze the light away and grow fat in greasy ease, but that they may have more time for books and music and drama and singing. And then outdoor plays and performances and the beauty of Maydays and the sweet and tender girl queen with the prideful young king walking by her side. And good health and joy and imagination among our children. And throughout the land a people alive with the sense of celebration—celebration of their past, their present, and their future—with festivals and choruses and orchestras and all the folk arts flourishing for the mutual stimulation and give and take among us every one!

For these are the decorations of life, the inspiration, the fire, and color and drive and depthful meaning of life. And in these days now it is no longer a matter of the pocketbook and gadgets of commerce, if it ever was, but a matter of the soul. It is the soul I'm talking about.

I am talking about the soul.

The Theatre Creative

Yes—the theatre critic said forlornly as he stretched his feet out to the fire—the American theatre is in a sad state of decline. The bold figures of high dramatic enterprise are all dead or fled and only the little traders in the temple are left alive. Indeed the temple itself throughout the width and breadth of this land has been torn down and a gaudy emporium, repeated in replica a thousand times, erected in its stead. So let us turn away from futile repining and go get our jobs in the entertainment industries of the movie and radio and television. For these are what the people want and pay to see and hear. The overwhelming facts assert it. You go get the job, I mean, I am too old.

For while the art of the theatre stands bankrupt, these other mediums through thick and thin continue to thrive. The bent of the times is different now and the theatre fails to fit in. The movies and radio and television do. Speed and machinery and mass-made entertainment are the go. The theatre is too slow, too unwieldy and expensive for value received. Its confines are now too narrow for the restless and high-powered American ambition.

Take the case of the leading American playwrights. Where are they? What has happened to them? For without good playwrights you can have no sort of theatre. They are the

first and foremost element that goes into its making. Call
the roll and they don't answer. A spade is a spade, and a
funeral a funeral. Most of them have left Broadway, gone
on a journey, turned to writing for these same mediums or
taken up the novel, or become poets if they are writing still.
True they come back, but only occasionally, and with ever
increasing delay between trips, with a play for Broadway.
And nearly every time the play they bring is weaker than
the one they offered before. Their energies and inspiration
have been stilled and scattered. Others have quit the game
altogether for real estate, brokerage business, life insurance,
law, teaching, editing, or what not.

And as they have failed,—the critic went on—so of necessity all the other theatre artists have failed and been denied
their proper chance. They have had to depend on the playwrights for material to work with, and the playwrights have
not come through. So these artists have been frustrated to
privation, and their hopes and plans and purposes gone glim-
mering on paper or died image-faded and wordless in their
heads. Think of the vast projects that Norman Bel Geddes
once dreamed of and schemed. Consider the visions and plan-
nings of Joseph Urban. Where are the actual accomplishments in the imaginative drama that Robert Edmond Jones
has spent most of his life trying to see realized? Nowhere.
None of these gifted men has been sustained and buoyed up
by a playwright and a talent and integrity equal or compara-
ble to their need. They still wait and will continue to wait
the genius they had a right to look for. By this time they must
know he will never come, not in their lifetime. No wonder
they too are having to turn to engineering, architecture,
and furniture designing, piddling some and making notes and
writing little theatre essays in their dismay and emptiness of
days, and all to ease themselves.

And if you're not convinced that the American theatre

is dying or dead, let me add a few final and more specific facts. There are today in New York City some seven or eight thousand actors, all waiting around, wearing out their skirts and trousers in some manager's office, or pitifully walking their shoe leather off on the sidewalks looking for jobs that never come. Some seven or eight thousand, mind you, when in any one season there are never more than a scant few hundred jobs available, and only for a few days or weeks at that, so small has the demand become, and daily becoming smaller. They live wretchedly from hand to mouth, borrowing money from this friend or that, picking up this crumb of hope here and there as best they can.

And the same thing applies to the young and unknown aspiring playwrights. Thousands of plays are written year after year—seventy-five thousand in the United States last year according to the figures I have gathered—and not one in five thousand ever gets a Broadway hearing. Maybe they shouldn't, of course. Most of them aren't worth the paper they're written on anyway. But why can't the best of them be heard, even in experiment? Because there is no place to produce them in. And if there were, the difficulties of production have become so great that you can find a manager only now and then who will take the risk. He is forever finagling for a sure-fire success. He cannot afford to experiment. Between the real estate and union demands the poor shivering author is stymied, and the play he poured his life's blood into is left to be eaten up by termites or silverfish or whatever it is that feeds on manuscripts.

Twenty-five years ago—my friend gloomily went on—there were some five thousand professional theatres and opera buildings thickly dotting the map of the United States. Hardly a town of any size but had its local playhouse. In them the best Broadway professional and stock companies offered the latest and finest in the world's theatrical art. Current European as well as American plays were given—oh, yes, along with the tripe too. And there were musicals and operas. Here Shakespeare, Moliere, Sheridan, Ibsen, Scribe, Maeterlinck, Rostand, Shaw and even O'Casey were shown. In New York City alone there were, I estimate, more than two hundred such theatre buildings. Boston, Chicago, Philadelphia, Washington, Baltimore, San Francisco, and other cities had their dozens. Where are they today? Gone, torn down. In the whole country there are less than a hundred left, and hardly twenty-five of them remain in New York. Yes, the theatre no longer has a home. So homeless it must die.

Well, that's the way the story runs—my friend, the discouraged critic concluded—and I see nothing that can be done about it except to say goodby and gone to it all and turn our minds to other things.

II

Although I tried to argue against the facts, my friend would have none of it. His mind was closed. And when finally I pointed vehemently to the work of the amateur theatre in America, or people's theatre as I like to call it, he threw up his hands in anathema and smote the air.

Now there's no doubt about it, the facts he unrolled were discouraging enough. And if there hadn't been another side to it all, I would have had to give in before him. But there is another side.

The trouble with this theatre pessimist as with all the others is that though their facts are logical enough their premise is all wrong. Their mistake lies in continuing to identify the American theatre solely with Broadway, when such identification is no longer possible. Twenty-five years ago it might have been true in the main. But it is so no longer.

The American theatre today is not on Broadway but

in the thousands upon thousands of amateur and non-professional groups in the hamlets and towns, in the granges, the high schools, the colleges, universities, trade union halls, army posts, and in the civic centers everywhere. It is the theatre of the whole vast United States. And I am thankful that this is so, thankful that the narrow confines, the bottle-neck of Times Square no more is sufficient for the clamor and urge to self-expression among our people.

Where there were once five thousand, (his figure) theatre stages in the country and all an extension of Broadway and its syndicalists, now there are twenty-five, thirty, even fifty thousand, built and created by the people themselves for their own needs, their feelings, purposes and vision. And here night after night they act and see acted and set forth in all sincerity dramas and stories of their own choosing and often of their own writing. Though many of these plays and their produc-tions are crude and uncomfortably naive, they are still their own and have an enriching meaning to them. And always the quality is improving.

Tonight as I write these words there are more plays being done in America than ever before. And there are ten times as many people seeing them as were seeing the Broadway product in those lamented twenty-five years ago. In the last twelve months alone there were more than four hundred thousand, nearly half a million, amateur theatre productions of plays in the United States. At least thirty play-agent firms —among them Samuel French, the Dramatists Play-Service, and Walter Baker—are engaged full time in handling the rights and royalties for this multitudinous business.

The American theatre is not dying. It is alive and flour-ishing as it never has been. Only the Broadway theatre is dy-ing. Nor is it actually dying, for that matter. It is only being whittled down to its proper place and size in the national scheme of things. And that is good for all concerned. The people's theatre is no longer an extension of Broadway. Rather the reverse. Broadway is a part of the people's theatre and only a part. The facts prove that and no more than that. And as Broadway has shrunk on down to the point where its twenty current productions are about equal to its needs and abilities, and as the professional playhouses, the old opera houses and academies of music have disappeared under the onslaught of the movies and machine-made entertainment, just so has this people's theatre proportionately increased.

So far as I know there has not been a single playhouse erected in New York City since the Ziegfeld Theatre was built there on Sixth Avenue and Fifty-fourth Street some twenty-five years or more ago. But what has happened in the "provinces"? In that time literally thousands have been built—from coast to coast and from the Gulf to the Great Lakes. In the last ten years more than a billion dollars has been spent on theatres and amphitheatres and equipment in the non-professional field. Here our young people are working away, shaping, building, creating and giving expression to the abundance of life and joy and the artist's urge that pulses in them.

I wish I could call the roll, telling about the countless groups and what they are doing—there in Seattle, at Stanford, in Wisconsin, Minnesota, the Dallas Little Theatre, the University of North Carolina, Loyola, Williams, Penn State, Texas, Iowa, Cornell, Cleveland, Pasadena, Dartmouth, Berea, Carnegie Tech, Vassar, Smith, Syracuse, Rollins, Swarthmore, Mount Holyoke, Washington and Lee, Amherst, Stephens, Hunter, down in Athens and the deep South where poverty and economics are supposed to put out the light, Miami, Shreveport, Little Rock, and on up to Indiana with its million dollar playhouse—but I have neither the space nor the time here. That is a thrilling and tremendous story in itself, separate and apart. And what makes it so thrilling and tremendous is that at last and for the first time in the history of our country the theatre is finally being recognized and used as a vitalizing and powerful force in the education, development, and culture requirements of our people.

Symphonic Drama

Many years ago I became interested in a Negro settlement on the outskirts of a certain southern university town. This settlement consisted of four or five hundred people. It incorporated into itself almost everything good and bad, cruel and hopeful, superstitious and factual to be found in any village below the Mason and Dixon Line.

Here were the turgid upboiling and rich manifestations of humanity with all their special intensity of emotion, wilfulness, and wild flarings of the imagination—manifestations which Negro folk life in America so fully provides. I dreamed and pondered over this settlement. I wanted to give dramatic expression to this environment and active milieu of life. I wanted to write a play about these people.

Certain decisions had to be made. A central gathering place must be established in the play—a place where the people would be brought in and where they could discharge their dramatic story message, where they could unload their personalities, as it were, in the scene and pass out and return to unload again.

What would the center be? First I thought of that gathering place of communal life, the church. But on consideration, it offered certain stiff and formal difficulties. Next I thought of the corner grocery store. But, owing to its pragmatic and definite purpose, I found it too narrow and confining. What about a barbecue stand? I could see the people eating there, hear their loud guffaws as jokes were cracked. See a quarrel being picked. There comes the strolling form of the law. But, no, that won't do. Too many representatives of Negro life, especially the more delicate and feminine side of its society, would be excluded.

I finally chose a boarding-house—a proper-sized boarding-house. And for freedom of movement and contrasting mass of bodies and lights and shadows I would need several levels of playing action. Therefore a boarding-house with a porch on it. And, too, there should be a yard and some shade trees —one shade tree—in front. People in the South like to sit under shade trees. The walls of the rooms in this house should be opened so that the inner workings of this dwelling as a habiting place for human souls could be depicted as the story required. Also why not a lean-to at the back into which we could progue our sight? It could be a level higher than the room in front of it. This was good. And a bed in it also —always a dramatic and creative property.

And if necessary I could bring in another small center of action—the local barbershop shack. Yes, that would be right. So off at the left of the yard I moved a tiny outbuilding where the seeking light could cast its interested eye now and then and discover to the audience whatever bits of action might be needed to further the story along.

And let a street cross at the right where the moody and restless life of the people could pass in emphasis and illustration as the play required. So now I had enough of a home, with intimate cells, in which the dramatic honeybee could work.

The scene had four playing levels then—the yard, the front porch, the main interior of the house, and the higher lean-to level at the rear. In addition, there were the playing spot of the little barbershop outbuilding and the highway of action along the road to the right.

In and around this boarding-house I now collected my characters, some seventy-five or a hundred of them, all representative of a cross-section of Negro life. Among them were a preacher, a mother or two, a granny woman, a voodoo doctor, several convicts, a harlot, a beautician, a sport, a blind musician, several day laborers, cooks, an undertaker, several pairs of sweethearts, a salesman of death insurance—and men, women and children. These last were in the main chorus figures. The theme I had in mind brought them all into being—and not the reverse.

What about the time? I must choose an hour and a day in which it would be natural for this Negro life to coagulate and congregate itself into such a setting. A Saturday night then. It must not be in winter, for then my characters could not do their stuff out-of-doors. So summer it must be—a warm summer night when one week's hard work had ended and another week's had not yet begun. At such a time the story germ would sprout quietly, develop normally, and break into a final bloom of explosiveness. Then after this, normal life would return to quiescence again and the play be over.

As I worked at the drama, I felt again and again that I was involved in the same sort of enterprise as a composer driving forward his composition for some eighty or a hundred instruments. The whole body of the work must be kept propelling itself onward by means of the individual instrumentations which came forward to personal fulfillment, returned and gave place to others, and they in turn likewise. Motifs must be developed, thematic statements made and exploited, and a ferment of symphonic creativity be kept brewing to self-realization. And all to be sternly controlled by the architectonic power of the story line. Whatever failed to advance the story would not be used. For, after all, drama is story-telling. Of whatever sort, it is storytelling in action. Of course a little functional and lyrical decoration could be indulged in now and then. But only beauty spots, as it were, to be tinted in on the face of the whole.

And the *idée fixe*, say, as in a Beethoven or Berlioz symphony, the sensed and felt and inner natural form, call it even the melodic line, whether submerged or surfaced—must control matters.

The story line was a creature alive indeed. And even as the will-o'-the-wisp, he lived in and inhabited the scene. There the little creature enters from the street. He moves about the yard. The house calls to him. He enters there. He takes possession of a room for a while, and the human beings indwelling there are disturbed and thrown into fits even at his galvanic appearance—an appearance called up out of their own deep desires and activities, their clashing wills and urges in themselves—just as the violins flutter and cry out in sweet stridency or joyful pain as the burden of the symphonic movement develops or comes to being in their vibrating and shaken bosoms.

II

I kept searching for a term of definition and interpretation to describe my play as I worked at it.

I found that in trying to express the inner lives and turmoilings of my Negro community I was having to call upon nearly all the available elements in modern theatrical art. And there were plenty of them. Folk song and poetry were needed here. Likewise the dance and pantomime and chorus voices. Even the mental speech of the grisly microphone and echo chamber could be used to get inside the soul life of some of my disturbed and vitalized people. Moments of horrification would call for masks. And ever there was the dynamic flow and modulation of light to accompany the human behavior at work. Light that would illuminate a volatile and advancing story point. And in that illumination the mind of the appreciator could read the message clear. The fabled fire in the Scriptures was like this light, the furnace fire in which the Hebrew children once stood all bright and glorified.

And always there was music—music!

"Music drama" didn't seem the right term for the play. "Ballad opera" it couldn't be. Nor "opera." "Festival play" was too loose and misnoming. "Lyric drama" lacked entirely. Finally "symphonic drama" seemed right. Yes, a "sounding-together" in the true meaning of the Greek word. The term seemed a little highfalutin, and I deplored that. But it was nearer what I wanted than anything else. And so I adopted it and have continued to use it for other like plays I have written since.

III

I found in writing this Negro drama that by the symphonic use of the various elements of the theatre, especially music, there came a freedom and fulness of possible story statement not otherwise to be had in dealing with large groups of people in action. Short cuts and intensifications could be quickly indulged in which the audience would accept without question. Conventions could be quickly established, and the story beginnings could be hatched out of an obstructive matrix without much ado.

In this kind of theatre, too, time could be telescoped through a symbol—even could become that symbol. Space might be compressed or expanded, say, like the breathing of some huge and delicate accordion of the mind. Tomorrow is already here. A voice of the inner chorus commentator out of the life of my Negro village could say so. And in the thickened moody and musically charmed environment, in the climate of credibility established, the audience would agree.

There was a nemesis in my Negro play. A huge and on-coming highway was being built by the white man across the earth and was aimed straight at this Negro settlement. The deep reverberations of dynamite exploding in the hills, clearing the way for this road, sounded ominously and constantly nearer as the drama proceeded.

Passions and hates and loves and fears and whorings were fecundating in this village. During the play murder was committed in the boarding-house. Then came the wham-wham of a policeman's stick, and the hoarse great voice of the Law was heard bellowing like Behemoth through the valley. Culprits and innocent ones ran this way and that in fear. The Golem tread of justice and retribution came nearer. The reverberations on the distant road sounded closer, louder. Nature herself became sick, upset, and violent. A fierce wind whoomed and whistled among the shacks in the valley and around our particular boarding-house. The limbs of the shade tree in the yard twisted and swung like a gesticulating maniac. A final and terrific explosion occurred in the street at the right. A pandemonium of shrieking and lamentations of the people rose in the valley! The moon dropped down the sky like a shot. And then, with the echoes falling away, the tumult and the terror died. The scene faded gently and musically out. From the darkness came a low and fervent chanted prayer of the persecuted and disordered people. A few heartbeats of time and no more, and the light swam up again.

The iron-snouted machine-age road had arrived. The nemesis was there. It had plowed its revengeful way through the settlement like a cruel steel coulter through an anthill. The old boarding-house had been pushed aside. The entrails of furniture and pieces of bedding spilled out along the torn earth. Because of the depravity, the sinfulness, and causeless misery of these sorrowful ones the road had taken its toll.

A dozen or more striped convicts were working, digging away on this road now, slinging their picks and bringing them down, and ever bringing them down in the white blazing sun. The heat of August shimmered across the land. "Lazy Lawrence" danced his fiendish monkey dance in the sun. The sweat poured down, the only cooling dampness in the world for the mourners on that road. On a stump to the left a guard squatted, drowsy, vapid, like a toad. The rifle in the crook of his arm kept alert, its muzzle warned like an eye, it threatened. The convicts dug on and on, their faces set down the infinite stretch of cruel road that reached from the rising to the setting sun. And as their picks came down against the earth with a thud, a husky desperate groaning chant burst from their baked lips, carrying on and carrying on over the long deadening hours of pain.

In this form of symphonic drama the convicts and the digging had become the road.

The form seemed right then for the expression of such group life, of setting forth the relationships of individuals and their fellows, of masses and crowds affected, energized and motivated as they would be by some centripetal idea and dramatic intent—some story of tradition, of folk inheritance and legend, some famous native character or group of characters splurging themselves forth out of their heritage.

IV

So I wrote the piece to the best of my ability. Then began the peddling of it for Broadway. I experienced to the fullest the torturous way to production so often endured by American playwrights. I would have been much wiser of course to have found some amateur group and perfected the production with them first. But no, it must be Broadway or nothing, I thought. I have learned better since. Some half-dozen managers were intrigued by the play, bought it and owned it in turn, paying five hundred dollars down, fiddling with the script six months and dropping it. For three years they did so. Finally one more foolhardy than the rest, a woman, undertook it.

The play arrived at the Cort Theatre on Forty-eighth Street in New York. From the beginning on that autumn night everything went wrong. Our prize exhibit of twenty-two choral voices in the pit, flanked by a drum and a clarinet to provide the basic musical folk-stratum, went dead on that opening night. All its fire was doused. All sense of Negro revival participatingness had vanished. It was a cold group, frozen, stiff, automatic, and unable to fuse itself into the body of the play. And yet Dolphe Martin's score of notated vocables was sure and eager and alive.

The actors likewise played separate and aloof solitaire. The voice of the Almighty (the white man's Law), which had been placed high in the scenery aloft by means of a loud-speaker, blew a fuse in the midst of its stern admonition to the struggling and wayward Negro villagers. The already puzzled audience broke into laughter.

And all the while there was to be no relieving intermission. I had been bull-headed on this point. This was to be a through train, like the train that took old Daniel away in the song, and there would be no stopping until it arrived at its final destination, either heaven or hell.

It was to be hell.

I walked restlessly up and down in the lobby of the theatre. I kept going out to the sidewalk to see how the weather was up the narrow canyon of the dark sky and then back listening, waiting for any sound of encouraging applause from within the auditorium. None came out. But a man came out

instead, irate, hot and bothered. He was a big fellow and to
my then disordered imagination looked like Goliath, and me
with no sling shot and only a heart for a stone.

"Play or no play," he said, "I'm going to smoke."

It was Bob Benchley, and I knew we were sunk.

v

Two days later word was received that Mr. Shubert
wanted his theatre come Saturday night for another show.
Trembling and afraid, I went over to see him. He was gra-
cious and humane and unsmiling.

"Your drama lacks entertainment," he said.

"But if we could only keep it going another week. Give
it a chance. Maybe it would catch on. It's a sort of new form,
you know. Atkinson's review was not bad. I have a wire here
from him praising it. And Mrs. Isaacs of *Theatre Arts* thinks
highly of it."

"I understand how you feel," he said, "but I already have
another show booked to come into the Cort right away."
His voice grew a little hard. "A full-length play without an
intermission is unthinkable. The audience won't stand for it."

"Won't sit for it," I corrected inwardly.

I looked at his emotionless face. There was something fa-
miliar about him. Then I knew. It was his snow-white collar
and his black exact tie. In the very play he was kicking out
one of the characters was a Negro mortician. Mr. Shubert's
collar and tie were identical with the Negro's and as solemn
and unfeeling. The office was a morgue then, and I was glad
to get away to fresh air. So *Roll Sweet Chariot* rolled out of
the theatre on Saturday night into silence.

VI

I tried this sort of symphonic drama a couple of other times on Broadway. Once the cool and loyal judgment of Cheryl Crawford, the enthusiasm of Harold Clurman and the Group Theatre, the fine direction of Lee Strasburg and the resilient and theatrewise music of Kurt Weill—all helped to mend matters. But they were not enough, and *Johnny Johnson* likewise was marked down as a failure. I still remember with appreciation though that the critics' circle gave it a tombstone vote of confidence for its obituary.

Then there was *Native Son,* which I co-authored with Richard Wright out of his dynamic and powerful novel of the same name. This play was symphonic in its use of music and musicalized sound effects especially. The undismayed personal dominance and theatricality of Mr. Orson Welles helped salvage the piece and drive it across to some sort of crippled success. It ran in New York for several months and then continued around on the road for a year or two. It is now being played in different parts of the world in various translations, and I hate to think that its meaning to foreign audiences is not its drama but its propaganda.

I have written several symphonic dramas away from Broadway and have had better success in staging them in outdoor theatres than in indoor ones. Down on lonely Roanoke Island in North Carolina Sir Walter Raleigh's colony perished in 1587. A hundred and twenty-one men, women, and children disappeared from the face of the earth without a whisper as to their fate. For many years I thought about this mystery as material for a symphonic drama. With local devotion and a great deal of WPA and Federal Theatre help we built an outdoor amphitheatre there close on the quiet waters of Roanoke Sound. And in a setting of yellow sands and live oak trees we opened *The Lost Colony* in 1937. The play is beginning its annual summer season and has already passed the 600th performance. Through these years hundreds of thousands of people have come to see this project in communal theatre and to hear the old English music, the folk song and hymn tunes of our musical heritage, and to see the native Indian dances—all part of the symphonic drama. The little fishing village of near-by Manteo furnishes us with many actors, New York likewise. They all meet here, more than a hundred of them, year after year, and put on this play, their play. And the miracle to me is that the box office has so far provided enough salary to give each participant a modest living wage.

Another symphonic drama already written is *The Highland Call*. It is designed for production in the Cape Fear Valley in North Carolina. This valley is a home and center of the Scottish settlement in the United States. And recently there among the tall pines outside the city of Fayetteville close by Fort Bragg we selected a site for our outdoor theatre. And here, before long, it is my hope, the story of the Scottish heroine, Flora MacDonald, with the music and ballads and dance of the early Scottish settlers in the New World, will be played nightly under the stars.

The Common Glory at Williamsburg, Virginia, is another example of this type of drama with which I have recently been working. This play covers six years in the life of Thomas Jefferson and is concerned mainly with his efforts to further the creation of democratic government in these United States. This summer will mark the seventh season of the drama. And so far it has been highly successful as regards attendance and box-office income. The policy of using local actors, strengthened by some Broadway professional ones, is used here just as in the case of *The Lost Colony* and the planned-for *The Highland Call*.

And there have been other symphonic dramas—*Faith of Our Fathers* produced in the beautiful outdoor theatre in Rock Creek Park, Washington, for the seasons of 1950 and 1951, *The 17th Star* produced at Columbus, Ohio in the summer of 1953 in celebration of the state's sesquicentennial celebration, and *Serenata,* a fiesta drama of old Spanish days in Santa Barbara, with Josefina Niggli, the summer of 1953.

And waiting ahead is *The Shepherd of the Isles,* the drama of that great humanitarian James Oglethorpe and his settlements of Georgia planned for production in a theatre to be built on St. Simon's Island in 1954. Then there is the story of the tenacious and pious pilgrims at Plymouth. After that, the drama of the trials and sufferings of the first settlers in that nightmare of terror that was Jamestown.

And up and down the length of California I have traveled, stopping at every old mission from San Francisco to San Diego looking for a site, a home for a future great passion play of the Southwest. It seems now as if somewhere in the quiet and brooding mountains of Ojai Valley a place will be found for building the most beautiful outdoor theatre in the world, and there under the dry and rainless stars the religious and inspiring story of the early padres in that wide land could be restated and relived.

VII

This type of drama which I have elected to call symphonic seems to be fitted to the needs and dramatic genius of the American people. Our richness of tradition, our imaginative folk life, our boundless enthusiasm and health, our singing and dancing and poetry, our lifted hearts and active feet and hands, even our multitudinous mechanical and machine means for self-expression—all are too outpouring for the narrow confines of the usual professional and killingly expensive

Broadway play and stage. But they can be put to use in the symphonic drama and its theatre. It is wide enough, free enough, and among the people cheap enough for their joy and use.

Playwright—to a Friend in Woeful Times

I was glad to get your letter and sorry to hear that you had been under the weather. I was sorry also to hear that you had just finished reading my patriotic play and had hurled the book with an oath across the room, just stopping short of lighting your fire with it. All vague and vacuous words, you say, something about an American dream. Well, now I hope with spring in full bloom and the drear-nighted January passed away, these mulligrubs which have infected you will be killed off by the warm light of summer and the "doleful doings" of your mind will give way to the persuasion of flowers and birds and trees and the rich profusion of life pouring out its sweet and everlasting miracle upon the land. That at least should help the naked thorn.

You say, too, you are fed up with your environment there —with its clang and clamor, its compressive stir of busy and failing lives, and wish you were out of it and back among the pines of Carolina.

I hear that sort of story often and remember my father's old saying about cows off yonder having long horns, or the grass being greener in another pasture, old sayings that fitted your case the day you left us for your future there just as they maybe fit you now that you want to come back again. And he would also say that where the grass is greener it takes more work to keep it cut. As for the social ways of a lot of the people around you there, the baiters and the beefers, the manikins and minikins with their psyches and their dogs, the ism-fanatics, the birth-control professionalists, the cultural center aesthetes clasped emptily together for comfort and for art—to list but a few you mention—well, they are to be found everywhere and you won't escape them by coming here. For as both Brigham Young and Schopenhauer have well shown, along with Solomon, desire is mighty and will prevail, and all kinds of people are forever being dumped into this world. Activity continues, and when love is off economics is on, and usually both are putting in full time together.

Yes, like a mighty tree, old life keeps pumping us up in sap from below to spill out as long as time shall last in rich fruitfulness at the top. If some of the twigs do freeze and die, the main and leafy wonder still goes on. And I wouldn't waste too much worry on these perverse and blighted twigs, either. They will rot and fall to the ground to add their pinch of fertilizer to the enrichment of the mystic bush above. This has always been true—as witness the million cold April-bud little poets, artisans, and inventors who have added their small mite to the big things that happen in the world. This is the process known and accepted in the Orient long before the western world was thought of, and we might do well to consider it. I refer you to the Hindu scriptures which can now be got in a cheap edition of Everyman's Library. Also Tagore's philosophical essays. You might draw some comfort from them. You know we used to talk a lot about these things when we were both students there at the university. I have discovered the books since then, and they help some in all the pain,—some but not too much.

II

Now, this all sounds a bit hardboiled and unsympathetic—
like a kind of let-things-wag-as-they-will philosophy, and
don't give a hang. I don't mean it that way. I believe that the
burning bush or willow tree of life—use what figure you
will—is endowed with the miracle of consciousness, of emotion, mind and will—and all of us its parts have the power
and the bounden duty to help it grow into the world as a
thing of beauty forever. That is not only the opportunity
and urge of man but his instinctive joy also. There are failings away all along the line of course like those you mention
above and like those we see every day in any forest. And it
has to be so because of an infinity of environmental and
heredity factors which can never wholly be made to behave.
But the main body of the tree, of humanity, does not fail and
never will, only the bitten twigs and sunless branches die.

And when you cry out in your middle-aged distress along
with H. G. Wells and others that all is confusion and despair
in a world of strife and you would, please suh, rest for it and
give over, I know you are wrong and hasten once more for
my own clarification and your encouragement to tell you so.
I have a sort of abdominal philosophy, an inner witness as it
were, that testifies even in the small hours to me that the
course of man is upward and not downward.

And even if it were not true, it ought to be, the ought
being the main thing for us. For in the first place man wills it
so and in the second it is the way all things in the large seem
fated to proceed. It has taken me a long time to throw off
the pessimism which our professors of rationalistic philosophy and science drenched me with as a student, and maybe
if you thought around a while you would find some of their
old wayward words still whispering to you from the "subconscious" dark.

In these latter days, to repeat, I have found a deeper wisdom than theirs among the Hindus, in certain of the New Testament scriptures such as the first chapter of *John* and the seventh chapter of *Romans,* and in Greek philosophers like Plato, Parmenides, Heraclitus, and Plotinus. All of these testify, feel, know, and affirm a righteous logic in the universe, a logos, a principle of goodness which nothing can destroy for man except man himself, and he will not do it because he cannot prevail upon himself to so deny himself. In particular and perverted cases, yes, but never in the main and vital body of the tree of humanity.

Do not all men of whatever creed or calling as a rule appeal to this goodness? It is their light, the guide by which they act and do their business—even making their claims to killing and crookedness in its name. Their ways of finding it are different, and in this difference they often mistake the lesser good for the greater, and as a consequence wars and killings and grievous things continue to happen among us. But these too will pass away—in a long time, a long, long time. Here the challenge is sharpest for our so-called educators and political leaders. Let them get busy and help to shorten that time and so save suffering, but not by graphs and tables and edicts from above. Oh, no! Only by the wisdom of an understanding and loving heart. How then, you say, can new hearts be given to these so diseased ones except by cutting out the old and inserting the new, and then the body dies? Apart from all cuttings, let that body die, as even Polonius himself would say. Thereafter we shall consider.

And then after deploring the condition of the world and your especial section of it, you say that you are wretched over the breakdown of American ideals in these latter days. Nay, you go further and declare that these woeful times have proved too clearly that the American system of thought, its democracy, its ideals, are an idle dream talked about a

great deal but never proved, and now with the avalanche
of totalitarianism rolling toward us we have nothing with
which to meet the enemy, no real defense against him. Here
you wax lyrical with pessimism and doubt. America has
never done anything high and ideal in the history of the
world, you say. We have always been a dog-eat-dog nation
if the truth were acknowledged, and before we can get anywhere we've got to recognize ourselves for what we are—a
selfish money-getting, sharp-trading land of usurers. A neurosis of materialism! We have no muscle, no stamina. Far
better if we had a hard mailed fist at this doleful hour. Ah,
and what have the foolish poets sung so long? you ask—
"When in the course of human events—," "Certain inalienable rights—," "Government of the people, by the people,
and for the people."

"Words, words," you say. Yes, and yet more words, even
my own, pleading as they will—

Out of the rich and deep-bosomed earth,
Mother of all, life-giving and bountiful,
Thou builder and thou leveler,
For thee these words.

Shall not the stones speak, the towering craggy trees
Watchfully waiting on the western hills—
The soft-reeded rivers, the valleys and the springs,
And all of man's making, the roads and the bridges,
Beams and girders and the reaching cables—
The walls and the towers, the fences and the wayfares—
Are these dead and voiceless things empty of meaning?

The scythe drops down, the hammer nerveless drops,
The plow and the shovel wait unused and still,
The weeds take them, the roots thread their sightless sockets
    through,
The handles shaped to human hands dissolve in dust,
And the fierce and clamorous strength that used them once,

That ditched and dug and builded with them there
Is gone forever in the tomb.
What then, shall their dreaming and their purpose all be lost,
The head of agony upon the pillow turned for naught?

Out of the tomb is there no voice now,
There by the low enclosing wall of quiet,
Silent in the evening's grievous hush?—
All is muted in the fresh upflaming morn,
All tongueless waits the lordly mountain top.

Shall these souls be bound in the tremulous chains of the starlight,
Or dust and ashes befoul the bright head of beauty—
O fading footsteps lost forever,
O eloquent lips and passionate hearts,
And gesturing final hands!—
Shall these forever be as if they'd never been?

Nay, cry out the roll call of their prideful names,
Wake with the reveille of our buoyant song
These that lie forgotten and foregone.
Now all our walking is the paths they trod,
Our speech their same shaped mouth and tuneful tongue,
Our gestures still the same strong-fingered hand,
Plucking the bouquets, firing the guns,
Building and shaping and creating in their stead.
So thus the dead do live in us again,
And we the living honorably may die.

I believe that, and I'm sure you are wrong—not because
you attack Jefferson, Emerson, Lincoln, and any multitude
of others, but because you attack the deep and human vision
by which we claim to live. America has done great things
and will do other great things, noble things. It's not all words.
And what great things beyond the dollar and the dime? you
ask with weary and doubting irony.

III

All right, then, the conquering of this vast wilderness of the western world. It was not an easy thing to do, but our forefathers did it—slowly step by step, ax blow by ax blow, and furrow by furrow. At first only the precarious hold upon the eastern fringes of this land was theirs. Then with incredible hardship and toil from father to son and to other sons they made their way inland, up into the hills, to the mountains, over the mountains, across the rivers and the plains to still other mountains north and south till another ocean three thousand miles away was reached.

And out of this wide and boundless struggle with nature a strong self-reliance was developed, untrammeled by any clan intrigues, fealties, and old-world loyalties of Europe. The mother country was far away, and day by day grew farther both in space and time and memory. And these her children, as is the course of things, came to be men in their own right and jealous of their hard-won prerogatives, feeling a proud ownership in the place and product of their toils. And as they depended on their skill, their industry and strength without appeal or favor from others, so did they grow to resent exploitation by any outside authority. It's true, as you in your present state of discouragement are quick to point out, these pioneers in conquering the wilderness did from the very abundance of the land and its resources set the habit of waste and carelessness which has come so evilly down to this day. We must remedy such mistakes and are doing it. Even here there is work to do instead of repining like the insect in the fable.

Then there followed the creation of the democratic ideal of government. Try as you will you can't laugh or sneer that off. For centuries men had dreamed of such an ideal, had written and preached about it—Confucius, Plato, Jesus, John

Locke, and countless others—but none had ever found the proper statement for it or the time and place to put it into practice. And when on that long ago day of June 12, 1776, the Virginia House of Burgesses adopted the Bill of Rights as finally drawn up by the leading thinkers of that colony, something new had begun among men. I believe that. With this basic statement made, the Declaration of Independence and the Constitution of the United States soon were derived.

Here at last and for the first time in the history of the world a system of government was begun, based upon the recognition of the absolute worth of the individual, which declared that each and every man is an ultimate reality in himself and as such has certain inalienable rights that go with being a man. Nothing shall take these rights away from him. And to protect him in these rights, and for this reason only, governments can be said to rightfully exist. He shall be secure in his person and the earnings of his hands and brain. No one shall unjustly imprison him or visit excessive punishment upon him. He shall be free to go and come as he pleases, to speak his mind openly and freely, to think as he pleases, and to worship his God as he sees fit.

These are self-evident principles, our forefathers said, and irrespective of color, creed, or previous condition of servitude, men everywhere instinctively know them as true. For after all, men are individuals before everything else. Is not their birth, their love, and their death their very own and nobody else's? Can they feel with another's hands, eat with another's mouth, or think with another's mind? Their very being is their own and theirs alone. Man is who he is and nobody else. Can a child grow into manhood lying in the arms of his father? Or a daughter be more than that on the bosom of her mother? They must grow up. In homely phrase, every tub must stand on its own bottom.

Democracy is a philosophy fitted to men full grown, men

who acknowledge themselves as morally responsible beings as well as free, and who accept the rights that go with that responsibility. They accept freedom in terms of responsibility and responsibility in terms of freedom.

IV

And now the abuses. There are plenty of them. Our vision still exceeds our accomplishments, our reach, our grasp. But thank God we've had that vision, we've had the reach, and day by day we are making progress toward answering the challenge of those living words. And we are doing it from these basic principles beneath, not blindly from above as is the case with too many governments known as totalitarian. Let us try to remember that.

And our pioneer leadership in the creation of this the machine age! For the first time in the history of the world this country has produced the ultimately perfect servant—call him the cotton gin, the gas engine, adding machine, electric motor, telephone, talking machine, radio, television, atomic power, or what you will. And we have conceived of and created these machines for the service of the individual, the democratic man, as a means of lightening his toil, freeing him from economic slavery for exercises of things of beauty and the spirit and not for uses of hate and death and destruction. We so conceive of them and will as long as our democratic philosophy remains deeply integrated into the bone and blood-beat of our life as it is now.

Here again the vision is being abused. Too many of our leaders continue to be contaminated by the urge to profit and the main chance only. But we must not despair. It takes time, a long, long time for the hypocrites, windbags, and blackguards to die. But ultimately they will receive their fitting reward and epitaph—death. No system works perfectly, whatever the first reaches of its dream may proclaim, and the challenge always is toward a more and more perfect fulfillment.

This growing of the mystic tree then into the nobility of full form is a long process. It cannot suddenly be flowered into the sky by any artificial propagation or stimulus. It has to grow from the deep roots below, and this a power-sprung Europe and Russia will learn when their crises are past. It is easy to fight wars, it is hard to dramatize peace. Democracy's business is with peace, even when the militancy of marching feet and gleaming bayonets is required.

v

No, I do not share your discouragement about our country. I am more keenly alive to its greatness now than ever before. All of this tension and trouble you speak of maybe had to come. It is the convulsion of a new order breaking through the world. And that new order, when the convulsion is finished, will be one nearer democracy than otherwise. It may be called by some other name, but when it comes the individual must have his rightful place in it, must be recognized for what he is—a free soul with certain inalienable rights and responsibilities, or else the convulsion will break out again. (There is some dark here where I'm whistling, but not a midnight dark.)

Humanity is on the march to freedom, not to slavery, and nothing will stop it. The winning of the wilderness here, the riving out of our constitution, the creation of the machine age, are steps toward that world freedom, and as we have been pioneers in the past so must we continue to be in the future. And not until the new international order, in which both individuals and nations have their rightful place, has come to pass can we count the victory ours. And we must strive to spare the blood and the tears of the innocent ones.

And in that new day this country will begin the fourth great adventure of its history—the adventure of culture. Art, literature, music, philosophy, and true science will flourish then as never before. We are ready for them, and you be ready, too. Let us both add our sap to the main and leafy wonder, calling out with Whitman—

"Give me, O God, to sing that thought,
  Give me, give him or her I love this quenchless faith,
  In thy ensemble, whatever else withheld withhold not from us
  Belief in plan of thee enclosed in time and space,
  Health, peace, salvation universal."

And herewith I send you another play of American history, a sort of call to the highlands ahead. You may throw it across the room in disgust like the other one, but in doing so you can only criticize my ability and not the honesty of my intent. Nor will you in any whit diminish the joy I have had in constructing the story and bringing back to life these characters of the long ago—with something of their faith, their vision, and their cheerful song. Bear with me and read it through if you can.

So farewell, and send me a copy of your new book when it comes out. Don't forget the Hindu scriptures.

Music in the Theatre

Some years ago I met Alexis Granowski, the great Russian director. He had just brought his Jewish Moscow State Theatre troupe from that city for a short season in the German capital. The night before our meeting I had seen one of his productions and was so taken by it that I got a theatre friend to introduce me to him. He listened with evident appreciation to my enthusiastic outbursts over the kind of musical theatre which he had created. "Yes," he said in thoughtful English, "I think the music drama or musical play offers greater opportunity than any other. I have been working in this kind of drama now for ten years and every day convinces me of it. The use of musicalized pantomime, speech, and facial expression can liberate all those imaginative overtones of human psychology which straight realism can never touch. By the use of music all sorts of conventions and needs which otherwise might obstruct and disintegrate a production to nothingness can be got around, and short cuts in scenery, properties, and staging methods can be obtained. It is easier to go straight to the heart of your story, to reach its inner expressive symbolism, and most vital meaning with music. You say you liked my production of *Two Hundred Thousand?*"

"Very much. And tonight I'm going to see your *Travels of Benjamin the Third.*"

"Yes. It is the same style as the *Two Hundred.* In fact,

as I said, all of our repertory is music drama. Have you anything like it in America?"

"No, we haven't—not yet."

"If I should ever be forced to leave Russia, America is the country I would go to to begin my theatre over again. Of all the nations of all the world America seems to me the richest in dramatic subject matter—conflicts of individuals, of types, of institutions and organizations—a land of boundless energy, color, music, imagination—in short, the most creative nation on the globe. I know something of your theatrical history—I have heard of a few of your pioneer workers like William Vaughan Moody, Percy Mackaye, and of recent years of Eugene O'Neill. Who else have you?"

"We have Maxwell Anderson in the poetic drama. He is beating down a path, many of us feel, which will lead toward a new expression of American genius. And there are Sidney Howard, Robert Sherwood, Phillip Barry, Marc Connelly, Elmer Rice—"

"Do any of them make a great use of music?"

"I'm afraid not."

"Do you?"

"In a small way I have tried. To me it is the most inspiring kind of theatre."

"No doubt of that," he reiterated. "And why America hasn't developed an authentic music drama—" throwing out his hands—"well, that is one of these mysteries of art. But I prophesy before the real genius of your country can express itself on the stage, music vitally integrated into the drama itself must be used.

"I have often wondered why America has never created a great Negro theatre? More than once, in recent days and under the present regime (Russian) I have seriously considered moving to America to try to help build a Negro musical drama. Think of the rich possibilities you have there

—the singing, the spiritual, the vivid religious ideology, folk-lore, the tall tales, the dramatic conditions surrounding that submerged yet marvelously gifted people."

"Some experiments are being made," I replied, "in Harlem, in Cleveland, Ohio, in Chicago, and in some of the larger cities. But they are only small experiments and nothing big yet has been done."

"Do you know Mr. Otto Kahn?"

"I've met him."

"He is here in Berlin now, and I was talking to him the other day about such an idea, and he offered to consider sub-sidizing a Negro theatre if I would come to America to head it. Well, it's a thing to think about."

I saw Alexis Granowski once or twice more. I was present at a meeting with him and a few others on the tragic night he reported that his theatre was dissolved by a command of the Soviet authorities. He remained in Berlin for a while, then moved to Paris where he later died. I never knew why he didn't come to America in accordance with this dream he had.

It has been many years since that meeting. Mr. Kahn has long since died. Many American plays have been born and knocked their way on to the storehouse. Several Negro theatrical groups have been organized and dissipated. Dozens of musical shows have been written, made their money, re-ceived a redressing via Hollywood, amused the public, and passed on without remembrance. And the American music drama seems only a little nearer an actuality than before.

But that little is encouraging. For there is a growing feel-ing on the part of American playwrights that such a drama needs to be. And in some of the productions like *The Green Pastures*, *Knickerbocker Holiday*, *Porgy and Bess*, and *Lady in the Dark*, and especially on the wide front of radio and television drama, progress is being made. And, too, in the great American people's theatre outside of Broadway (the real American theatre now) more and more attention is being paid to the use of music in plays—especially in what I like to call symphonic dramas, those outdoor festival and historical plays now springing up all over the land—and someday not too far off the complete, vital use of the musical drenched word, rhythmic acting, and poetic speech no doubt will find embodiment and statement for a fervent and national audience.

I once heard Eugene O'Neill say, in reference to *Lazarus Laughed*, that the theatre would become a powerful force in American life only when some method was hit upon whereby the audience could participate in the performance somewhat as a congregation does in the ritual and service of the church. Whether this is true or not I don't know. But if one remembers the power of music in religion and what religion would be without that music, is it not likely that a people's drama without music just so is lacking one of its most powerful and vitalizing elements?

The Lost Colony: A Dialogue at Evening

(*The critic and the author are strolling about the amphitheatre grounds waiting for the play to begin. The twilight is coming down.*)

CRITIC: (*As they stroll.*) This project must have been an undertaking. (*He gestures toward the outdoor theatre near by.*)

AUTHOR: It was.

"What with that huge stockade around the fort, and the blockhouse, the chapel, the cabins, the amphitheatre, the stage, the dressing rooms and all."

"And the water system, hot and cold."

"That, too. It must have been a lot of work."

"It was, and a lot of folks did it."

"How many people would you say have been involved in the project?"

"Counting the workers, the actors, the technicians, and the citizens of the island, I should say about a thousand. Maybe more from first to last."

"Remarkable. It's a real community endeavor, isn't it?"

"Yes."

"But a little puzzling to find a venture like this down in a lonely country and so far from civilization."

"I don't know about that."

"About what?"

"About being so far from civilization."

"Hm-mn. Well, I mean so far from any big city. Norfolk is the nearest large town, isn't it?"

"Yes, about ninety miles away."

"That's what I thought. Where do your audiences come from?"

"They come from everywhere, like you and me."

"Yes, but I have a sort of professional reason for coming. I am a critic."

"The people come unprofessionally and because they want to see the show."

"Do you plan to run it year after year?"

"Yes, that is the intent of those in charge. We will continue it as long as the public will support it. I hope it will be going fifty years from now."

"I hope your hopes will be realized, but—" (*Staring off across the sound at the solitary Wright Memorial and the sand dunes in the distance.*) "It's a lonely country all right. Look at that water there in the sound—motionless, smooth as glass. Life stands still."

"But sometimes it cuts up."

"What?"

"The sound."

"You wouldn't think it. How do your New York actors like it here?"

"Most of them want to come back each year."

"And how do they get along with the natives?"

"After a few weeks you can't tell them from the islanders."

"What do the people do for a living here?"

"They farm a little, hunt, fish, do coast guard work, and in the summer put on the play and take care of the people who come to see it."

"And now about the play itself. How did *The Lost Colony* come to be produced in the first place?"

"I hardly know. I suppose it was because the people on Roanoke Island wanted it and worked for it. For a long while they had held some sort of local celebration off and on each August 18th in honor of Virginia Dare's birthday."

"Virginia Dare?"

"In the school books it tells how she was the first child born of English parents in the New World."

"I remember now. It has been so long ago."

"Yes, we all forget. That's why plays are written, so we won't."

"Perhaps. And then?"

"Well, the island people took the initiative in the matter. Led by our local Mr. D. B. Fearing and aided by Mr. W. O. Saunders, an editor from Elizabeth City (that's a town up in the mainland) they all set about preparing plans for a 350th anniversary celebration to memorialize Sir Walter Raleigh's lost colony and Virginia Dare. One of the plans was to hold a nationwide beauty contest to select the girl who should play Virginia Dare. At that time they didn't know, nor did I, that when the play came to be written she would be a baby and remain so. In all our minds was the legend that she grew up to be a beautiful maiden, fell in love with the Indian chief Manteo's son, married him, and became the mother of a brave race that somehow evaporated into thin air.

"As Mr. Saunders, Mr. Fearing, and others went on with their work, I who had always been interested in the romantic and tragic story of these early colonists joined with them. But our combined efforts produced little more than pledges of money and cooperation, and with the deepening of the depression they amounted to nothing. Then came the W.P.A. and saved us. Mr. Fearing and his helpers got a project approved to build the theatre, and I set about writing the play. With the aid of Congressman Lindsay Warren,

25,000 memorial fifty-cent coins were minted by the United States which were sold to collectors for a dollar and a half each. Through this means some funds were raised to pay the necessary proportion of materials for the project. And so we were started. But only started, for as the size of the production grew the need for more money increased. The night we opened we were deeply in debt. At least Mr. Fearing and certain local business men were."

"And the production paid out?"

"Yes, it has finally done so."

"You were lucky."

"We all were. If it hadn't been for the W.P.A. and the Federal Theatre—"

"Well, we can leave that out. You know how my paper feels about the New Deal and the boondogling gravy train. And now what do you consider to be the main factors in the success of the play?"

"The main reason was that our business manager and key man, Mr. D. B. Fearing, was a confirmed and energetic optimist. No sight of bad luck or fear of failure could stop him. Also another reason was that the local people were interested both as helpers and as active participants in the show. Then we had a fine and understanding director in Mr. Samuel Selden, a devoted builder in Mr. Albert Q. Bell, and a gifted newspaper man in Mr. Ben Dixon MacNeill who throughout the first summer kept writing vivid and human interest stories about the production. And finally the music, color, and movement of the play itself attracted the public. And those who came kept passing the word along to others. These were the main reasons, I suppose—not forgetting the technicians and actors, of course."

"I notice in the program here you call *The Lost Colony* a symphonic drama. Is it because you have music in it?"

"No, not primarily. I have used the phrase to describe one

or two other plays I've written. It's not a perfect-fitting term maybe, but the best I can find, better I think than music or musical drama. In the original sense it means 'sounding together.' That is, all the elements of the theatre working together—words, music, song, dance, pantomime, masks, mental speech, and so on."

"It's something new, isn't it?"

"I have been hoping there is something new in it. But I guess after all it's pretty much as old as drama itself. The Greeks and the people of medieval and Elizabethan England produced outdoor plays like this. And years ago Percy Mackaye wrote and produced masques and pageants somewhat like it."

"Do you call it a pageant or a play?"

"A play. For it tells a story, and the characters are individuals, not types, as is usually the case in masques and pageants. There is a conflict of wills, a goal—a story-line continuity."

"Do you think the idea will spread and other localities will produce such plays?"

"I hope so. It seems to me there is a great chance for this kind of drama in America. This is a vast country full of legends and rich in story and song—all waiting to be used. And with the convenience of the automobile there is no reason why large audiences cannot be drawn to any place if there's a colorful and interesting show to be seen. And there's something about a production outdoors that seems to fit the temper of the American people—their mind and athletic muscle-power—maybe all people for that matter. Within the next few years I hope to see hundreds of summer dramatic festivals and productions scattered over the land from coast to coast. That would be one more way of making our people's lives vivid and happier. Then maybe we would begin to have a real people's theatre."

"I've heard a great deal of talk in my time about a people's theatre. What do you mean by it?"

"I mean a theatre in which plays are written, acted and produced for and by the people—for their enjoyment and enrichment and not for any special and prime profiteer motive. Then when the country becomes theatre-minded, the level of taste and appreciation will gradually rise higher and higher. And some day the mountain peaks of drama—men like Aeschylus, Lope de Vega, and Shakespeare—will erect their lives on the solid base beneath. As long as the American drama stays bottled up in the narrow neck and cul-de-sac of Broadway we can expect nothing better than what we have. I don't mean bottled up exactly, for already groups and sections of the country are turning their backs on the professional theatre and beginning to write and produce their own plays and the plays of others in a style equal to the best. For instance, the finest production of *The Cherry Orchard* I ever saw was at the University of Iowa some years ago."

"But surely you don't think the amateur theatre can measure up to the high standards of Broadway generally?"

"I don't know how high the standards of Broadway are generally, but the amateur theatre not only can measure up to them, but will, and more and more so as time goes on. The decentralization of the theatre has already set in."

"I don't share your enthusiasm there. Nothing bores me so much as an amateur play. Frankly that's why I'm not so sure I'm going to like *The Lost Colony*. From the list here it seems there are too many amateurs in it."

"They're not professional theatre people, that's true. Most of them have other jobs to do and they act for the pleasure in it. I think they're wise. When you consider the thousands of young people wearing out their fathers' shoe leather tramping the fruitless pavement of Broadway, and think of the fine things they might be doing back in their home neighborhood or town—"

"Frankly I think you are unfair to Broadway. You've never looked at it justly nor given it a real try. You ought to, you know, for your own sake as a writer."

"Oh, I hope to continue writing plays for Broadway now and then."

"But that's not the way to do it. You must throw yourself whole-heartedly into it."

"I've thought a lot about that, too."

"And what sort of answer did you arrive at?"

"This." (*With a gesture.*)

"Oh, well—" (*Looking at his watch.*) "It must be about time for the show to start."

"It is." (*He stares off at the wide western sky.*)

"Are you planning any other productions like this?" (*They turn.*)

"One I've thought about a great deal is to be in western North Carolina—that is, if we can find some business men up there willing to take the financial risk. I want to see a beautiful outdoor theatre built there on a mountain top close to the stars. And with the music, song, ballad, and dance of the people as material to work from, a colorful and inspiring play can be done. Already I imagine great crowds of people coming from the south and from the north, moving along the skyline drive of the eastern world, all coming to see it."

"Aren't you a bit optimistic in your seeing?"

"It's nothing but a dream, I know. But some day—"

"Well, good luck. (*As a great diapason of sound suddenly breaks across the twilight.*) There, I hear the organ. Sounds rather nice."

"It sounds wonderful to me."

(*They go up toward the theatre.*)

Dramatizing Our Heritage

Last night I was reading that great trilogy of the ancient Greek dramatist Aeschylus, "Agamemnon," the "Choephori" and the "Eumenides," and I read too the comment of the illustrious German scholar, Dindorf—to the effect that this trilogy was perhaps the greatest production ever put forth by the creative spirit of man.

Maybe the scholar exaggerated. I don't know. But I do know that one of the reasons for the splendor of this literary work was that the author loved his subject, found it important. Aeschylus loved Greece and the heroes of his country's past. And in writing about his native land and these heroes, with the devotion he did, he the more kept alive the greatness and importance of both.

Now I along with many another—and I am sure this applies to a vast number of our people too—have sometimes found it hard to keep faith in my country. Too often I have not admired our leadership. Actually at this hour many of us are asking, what has happened to our leadership? But whatever our present statesmen and political leaders may lack, I have felt from my earliest boyhood that the principles of democracy which underlie our form of government are identical with the principles of truth and are therefore inspiring, enriching, and life-giving as the truth itself.

Yes, as time has passed, I have come to believe that our American heritage, our way of life as an ideal, possesses the righteous reality of a true religion.

And so it is that in these days of crisis—and I don't know when there were not times of crisis—I find myself turning back more and more to the elements and constituencies of our early democratic philosophy. I find myself turning for aid and sustenance to the pioneers and forefathers who helped define and state and bring forth into living terminology these ideals that are the root of our faith. I find myself going back to the early days of our nation's history, trying to put my ear in tune, as it were, to the speaking of these thinkers and leaders.

And just as in Greece her literary workers reinterpreted her heroes—told and retold the story of Ulysses, of Menelaus, of Agamemnon, of the beauteous gods and goddesses in the rosy-fingered dawn, and with each interpretation raised them into more vivid and inspiring reality—just so it has seemed to me that we in this nation should seek to interpret and reinterpret, to dramatize and redramatize our heroes—the pioneer figures, the explorers, the statesmen, the builders—men like Franklin, Washington, Jefferson, Adams, Lincoln, Woodrow Wilson, Edison, and Burbank. For as we work to make them live again, so much more will they and their best virtues live in the lives of our children and the generations of the future—generations who in turn can reinterpret and redramatize them for their children.

I don't mean that this is ancestor worship. I simply mean that if we can make real and manifest and dramatic in our thinking, feeling and doing the lesson and significance of our forefathers and leaders, just so much stronger and more stimulated can we be in facing the tasks that lie ahead of us.

And in moments of weakness as now, times of uncertainty and wandering as now, we can look back for a moment to these historical figures standing there in a close-up actuality, can cup our hand to our ear and listen to Washington's words riding on the wind as it were—hear him saying—"Observe good faith and justice toward all nations."—"Cultivate peace and harmony with all."—"Religion and morality enjoin this conduct; and can it be that good policy does not equally enjoin it?"—or hear the ever-encouraging voice of Jefferson declaring, "We stand for the equality of men, for the freedom of men, the responsibility of men."—"The purpose of the state is to see that the talents of its citizens reach their fullest expression each and every one."—"A nation can only be as strong and as healthy as its citizens are strong and healthy."

And thus it will be that from a backward look and a backward listening we can turn squarely to the future and face that future more reassured, more certain of the way we should and must go, of the things we should and must do, of the leadership we need to take and must take!

Jamestown—Thoughts for a Symphonic Drama

After Sir Walter Raleigh's tragic and futile attempts to found a permanent English settlement down on Roanoke Island (1584 to 1587), he turned his holdings and interests in the New World over to the Virginia Company headed by the great London merchant, Sir Thomas Smith. In 1607 the Company sent out its first colony, consisting of three ships, the *Susan Constant* (of 100 tons, carrying 71 persons), the *Godspeed* (of 40 tons, carrying 52 persons), and the *Discovery* (of 20 tons, carrying 20 persons)—a total of 143 people.

On May 13, 1607, they landed on this shore and began here where we stand today the first permanent English settlement in the New World. The struggle of this early colony is too well-known for retelling. Suffice it for sorrow and pride to say that it endured every conceivable discouragement, pain and suffering. Before the year was gone more than half its members had died in this swampy land.

In 1609 a fleet of nine vessels sailed from Plymouth with about 500 more colonists. But prior to their arrival the handful of desperate settlers here on Jamestown Island had had to make their peace with the Indians and had scattered to live with them in a sort of fraternity of bondage to keep body and soul together. But the braggart and brave John Smith with a few followers still held on here in the fort. By this time Smith had become the supreme commander and governor of the place—a place of desolation and despair.

Then in May, 1610, a hundred and forty men and women arrived from England by way of the Bermudas to replenish the colony. But they brought little food with them.

Starvation soon set in—the decision was finally made to abandon the colony—the same tragic decision which had been made by the Lost Colony at Roanoke Island farther south some twenty years earlier. But by fateful chance the fleeing settlers were met down the river by Lord Delaware arriving with provisions. The colony was saved.

From then on it had its ups and downs. But slowly, ever so slowly, the tide of human life pouring in from England gradually overcame the devouring capacity of death in the wilderness. Just as an encompassing and swallowing flood is overcome by sandbag after sandbag being thrown into the crevasse, so finally the heaped-up bodies and sacrifices here became so numerous, piled so high as it were, that death in its flood was finally defeated and hemmed back.

In 1618 when Sir Walter Raleigh was awakened in the early autumn morning in the Tower of London by the minister of God and piously told that his last day on earth had come, he must have marched more bravely to face the headman's insane ax knowing that at last he had lived to see his dream come true and here in the New World was being built permanently and for all time an "English nation." And in the following year, July 30, 1619, as a sign of that permanence, the first legislative assembly in the New World was convened in the old church on this spot, and self-government in the world was having its beginning.

So the colony's flickering feeble life strengthened daily

into the more healthy pulse of normal bloodbeat. The fields
spread themselves out onto the mainland. Plans and purposes
came more certainly to be, and many a practical endeavor
flourished. A sum of money, for instance, was raised and land
purchased to build a school for the unlettered savage. But
these prospective Indian students failed to glimpse in time
the true value of the enlightenment being prepared for them,
and on March 22, 1622, they and their parents rose in fury
and slew nearly 350 colonists out of a total population of
some 1,250. However, the survivors finally rallied, stopped
the Indians and drove them back into the forest. They buried
their dead and went doggedly on with their appointed
lives.

In 1644, April 18, occurred the second Indian massacre—
300 English settlers being killed. But by this time the population had grown to several thousand and was safe from anni-
hilation.

In 1676 occurred the first armed rebellion in the cause of
liberty in the New World—young and fiery Nathaniel Bacon
rising against the oppression and malfeasance of Sir William
Berkeley, the Governor. Jamestown was burned in the fighting, and young Bacon died soon thereafter of exposure and
fever and squared his account with God rather than the
governor. Sir William then marched back and took possession of the ruins, captured a number of Bacon's rebels and
hanged them and finally restored peace. One of the rebels
hanged was William Drummond, Governor of North Carolina, the only chief executive of a state ever to be executed
in America. Then in 1698 the Statehouse here was accidentally
destroyed by fire. And in 1699 an act of the General Assembly was passed, moving the capital to Williamsburg.

So Jamestown was left to darkness, to forgetfulness, to
the bats, the rats, the silence of the turning days and nights
and the ever-changing seasons—until on a day generations

later the tender care of the women of Virginia came and brought its healing touch of resurrection and remembrance.

II

In studying the history of this hallowed place as subject matter for a play, I have come to the conclusion that neither the more publicized John Smith, nor Christopher Newport, nor Sir Thomas Dale nor the proud Sir William Berkeley, nor Sir George Yeardley, nor the Reverend Mr. Buck, nor the faithful Reverend Mr. Hunt nor any councilman nor Burgess—no one of these was the hero of this the first permanent settlement—though each and all were brave and heroic and suffered enough for any overflowing measure of our praise.

The real hero of Jamestown, I believe, was a retiring Englishman named John Rolfe. Not much has been written about him. I have no pamphlets and biographies and data to prove my contention. Rather I have had to make my conclusion somewhat from the drift, the tendency felt and seen through the whole saga of this settlement. These signs point indubitably to this man.

As a youth there in his native England, Rolfe was fired to Sir Walter Raleigh's dream of the New World. He yearned to come with the first settlement to Jamestown. But he was in love at the time with a young English girl, and she didn't dare that dreadful journey. In 1608 they were married and soon thereafter they both did dare. They embarked for Virginia. The story of the nightmare of storm which was their voyage was written down by George Somers, a poet and fellow-passenger. His account is one of the most powerful and beautiful pieces of writing in the English language. It served as a basis of inspiration, the scholars say, for Shakespeare's famous storm description in the play, *The Tempest*.

At Bermuda a baby was born to the young couple. It was christened Bermuda, lived only a short while and was buried there. After some eight or nine months' work on new green timbers hewn from the forest, two small ships were constructed by the colonists, and they sailed again on their way to Jamestown, arriving there in the famous starving time of 1610. In the meantime John Smith had returned to England because of an injury received in a gunpowder explosion.

Now for many a long year the colonists on this island had had a dream that lured them like the enchanting will-o'-the-wisp—a streak of golden fire in their imagination—the dream of wealth in the hills to the west of here. But John Rolfe was one man in the colony who resisted the lure. He turned his back on this false enchantment and set to work digging in the soil, growing crops, not digging for gold. Finally in 1612 he perfected a new variety of tobacco as well as a process for curing it. And tobacco as a medium of exchange soon became the solid fact on which the colony was permanently founded.

In this same year the unrelenting wilderness carried off Rolfe's young wife, Elizabeth. In the spring of 1614, two years later, he and the Indian maid, Pocahontas, were married here in the old church—or in the church that stood on this spot.

Like the story of so many brave spirits, the tragic martyrs who perished here, that of Pocahontas was a moving one. I see her as the first person in the New World to feel the shame of race—and thousands have so felt it since. Before the white man came, she, along with her brothers and sisters, must have looked up at their earth-shaking father Powhatan, emperor of the western world and ruler of limitless lands, with fear and dread and wonder. And it must have been a bitter education for this girl gradually to realize that her father and her people in contrast to the white man—the white man with his guns, his thundering cannon, his great ships, his compasses and gadgets, his mirrors, his shoes and stockings, and gaudy dress, his axes and saws that could cut trees and make lumber as you watched—to realize that compared to the white man her own people were indeed poor creatures of freeze and flood—pitiful, benighted, woods Indians.

And in place of her childish beliefs in devils of the forest, in the grim and terrifying medicine man and his vengeful gods, she learned the radiant teaching of Jesus of Nazareth.

I can see her walking here by this river in the evening, as she talks to John Rolfe in her sweet and broken English, asking her eager questions about the ways and thinkings and beliefs of the white man. And as her love for John Rolfe deepened and his for her, her heart must have been torn with many wrenchings of loyalty and disloyalty, of fear and pride and shame and hope—the turmoil of a young and sensitive soul caught in the tragic dilemma of denying her race.

So though John Rolfe was the true hero of Jamestown, Pocahontas, the Indian girl, was the true heroine. The story of these two young people remains one of the most beautiful in our American inheritance. And here today we honor them. We repeat their names, we bow our heads in memory of their short and beautiful and anguished love. And some day I hope to see their story as I have conceived it in dramatic form put on in the amphitheatre we are now building in the woods of Williamsburg.

In 1616 John Rolfe took his young wife and their tiny son Thomas to England, arriving at Plymouth June 12, 1616, six weeks after the death of Shakespeare. She was presented at court, and a masque of Ben Jonson's was performed for her benefit. The paunchy, unstable King James paid homage to her, and sour and embittered old John Smith—now a sort of down-and-outer there in London—came to kiss her hand.

Stricken ill of smallpox, Pocahontas died the next year, 1617, and her body lies buried there in the little church at Gravesend 3,000 miles from home.

But the dream of the New World haunted John Rolfe even in his grief, and he soon made his way back to Virginia. Here again he set to work tilling the soil, building, laying out fields, showing by both word and example the glory of work—work with the hands, with the heart, with the mind —work in the earth. Make the earth flower, make it produce. For out of the earth comes man's sustenance, his dreams and his salvation, his inspiration—rising up from so lowly yet rich creativeness and reaching toward the stars above.

It is in John Rolfe's philosophy of work that his greatness and true heroism lie, that he becomes the real hero of Jamestown. In him was represented the essential character of the English race. In him was illustrated once more the reason for England's success as a colonizing power in the world. She has been a nation of men who worked.

Consider by contrast the case of Spain. Spain was avid and ravenous for silver and gold and jewels—just as so many settlers in this first colony were greedy and avaricious.

The New World meant that to Spain—treasure. She found it in plenty in Mexico, in Peru, and fetched it home in her thick-bottomed ships. And this gold, this unearned increment, this wealth, corrupted the nation. It was not an earned wealth. Man must earn what he uses and then he will know how to use what he earns—thus said and did John Rolfe.

It is fitting then that we honor these two—John Rolfe who exemplified in his character the truth that a life of a people, the life of a nation, can be built for endurance through service, through the joy of work. And honor to beauteous and tender Pocahontas who loved this man, who strengthened him in life and like him made the final sacrifice for the dream of a nation which is ours.

It is fitting too that in these grounds along this river there is a monument to John Smith and a monument to the Indian maid, Pocahontas. But it is not fitting that there is no monument to John Rolfe.

Let us build one.

In the massacre of 1622 John Rolfe was murdered by the Indians in his fields across the river, and no man knows to this day where his body was laid.

A Figure for Drama

His hands are big, his face is big-featured, his level eyes are wide-spaced, honest and penetrating, his eyelids don't blink much.

His lips are slightly heavy, not beautiful, not ugly. His mouth is not too attractive—he has suffered much from unhappy teeth.

His hair is gray and grizzled. He is getting on in age but is in the prime of his strength. He is still resilient and buoyant-souled. And never will he curse the hour he was born, saying, "let that day be darkness, let no man remember it."

For his imagination is outward and practical, not inward and self-aware.

There is no subconscious pool of melancholy or moodiness in him which can be beaten up to froth and hysteria.

He is in and of life, enrapt and happily harnessed in it. Give him length of years enough and he will be the American mighty eagle.

And he is a good man, a yea-saying man—one over whom and in whom hangs the eternal imperative of duty, the everlasting monition of right and wrong.

His ambition is boundless but it is right—an ambition worthy of the man—a determination to create a just government whose throne is in the hearts of men. And he must in order to succeed be as ruthless as any tyrant. Nothing is to deter him from his goal.

Even as a young officer of twenty-three he had ordered the hanging of deserters from the ranks of his lawful forces out on the frontier.

He is more than a man of sturdy strength and craggy lasting power. In him is another quality, the quality of Addison's Cato, noble gentleman.

And behind his actions are the principles in which he believes—the principles on which our nation is founded. From his diaries and letters and speeches his credo can be read.

What he is is what he does, and what he does is what he believes. There is no chasm in him.

II

He believes that a nation is necessarily like a man in its responsibilities and its moral obligations to the world. This is his general and over-all political philosophy. And in his struggles to found the republic strong he gives forth the statements based on this philosophy which will echo solidly and inspiringly in men's spirits through generations ahead.

He believes that a Divine Providence rules the universe— and that man by good actions, sound judgment and love of his fellowmen can come near this Providence, be in line with it and receive its protection. And thus he will the more nobly and safely complete his own life.

For him duty is a universal commandment, and he believes that when it is once felt and understood, a man should obey this command at all cost. For if he does not obey it, he will be going contrary to the divinity of both Providence and his own nature.

To shirk one's duty is to him the cardinal sin. Through all

his writings the word duty is an insistent and beating refrain.

He believes in strong leadership for the people lest the mass of men by their contrary passions, appetites and jostling for advantages run amuck.

His ideal is a strong central government founded on righteousness and justice.

He believes that a nation's continuing greatness must depend in the main on the genius of its most gifted sons. These he feels should be especially educated and trained to accept public responsibility. In this he is the cavalier Englishman, the aristocratic Virginia gentleman.

He holds that the evil of slavery must as soon as possible be eradicated, and he urges too that the ignorant body of both Negroes and whites be subjected to education and training for citizenship even as they must be controlled by the strong hand of a just authority above.

He believes that men by nature instinctively tend to co-operate one with another—if for no other reason than for mutual advantages of safety and trade.

He believes that war is the scourge and tragedy of man and must be eliminated from the world if that world is to be healthy and virtuous and rich and happy. And in the eradication of war each nation has its cooperative part to play with other nations.

He believes that property is a badge and proof of an individual's reliability and sturdiness as a citizen. Therefore, be thrifty, accumulate property.

He believes that a man's word or promise is his bond and that deeds, writings and titles are no more than an affirmation of that fact.

He believes there is no substitute for character, and character will prove itself in positions of responsibility in government. Thus men can grow, develop and become strong upholding piers for the Republic.

He has no patience with deadbeats and patronage hunters. When such barnacles threaten to encrust the ship of state they should be sternly scraped away.

And he believes in building things. He is a builder, whether of roads, canals, houses, farms or a new nation. He is our first master-builder.

And as a builder he is straining far ahead. He sees the coming of new ways and means of doing things—a science of agriculture, inventions of machinery, cranes and lifting levers, methodologies and easier ways of moving mass materials.

And like Franklin and Jefferson he turns his attention to the creation of tools to ease man's sweaty labor. In him are the urge and the genius of the machine age which some day will be—the engineering genius of the American people—called into being by the challenge of great rivers, of vast mountains and burning plains and floods and prairies where man must go and live and do his work.

And he believes in the arts—especially the arts of music and of drama. No man in public life loves the theatre as he does. These arts are the sweetening and refreshing ingredients of a people's life, he says, they should be encouraged, practiced, cherished.

And out of his good health he believes that life is a fine thing, and joy and delight are to be had from living it to the full—living it as becomes an honest and responsible man.

What a figure for drama! Where is the playwright who will put George Washington on the stage in all his strapping vitality?

III

And bitter is the morning and drear in December there by the wide Potomac River. The wind is sharp and it is cold,

cold in December. Grief is everywhere. Old Billy Lee says
so, and Billy should know. For he has been his master's body
servant and friend and adviser for thirty years or more. And
by the river Billy is mourning—making his lament, and the
slaves are mourning with him—all going down the hill to
make the tomb ready to receive their master.

There are a dozen or more of them, men and women, walking in single file and carrying hoes and rakes, an ax or two
and a mattock. They are dressed in old heavy clothes against
the biting cold, and are singing mournfully as they move
along with bowed heads—singing in their queer dialect—

> "Let earth in dust and ashes hide
>   Before the awful sign,
> The moon run down in purple stream,
>   The sun forebear to shine!
>   Then grieve, grieve, grieve
>   For death's a hard trial."

Far away the sound of a great gun is heard. The slaves
shudder and moan and look fearfully off. They carry on
their song—in wordless harmony now—as they march on
down the hill. Billy Lee, the last in the line, comes limping
along. He also carries a rake. He stops and leans on the handle
like a walking stick, as he listens to the echoes of the gun. He
stands there listening. He begins talking to himself, his pain
and anguish rising into words—words musing and sorrowful:—

Yeh, yeh old death's walking round and 'bout now, and
po' Missus is grieving. Sitting there in her chair bowed down,
her head all low, she's grieving. And the slaves is grieving.
Their hearts is slam broke in two. And up in Alexandria the
people's hearts done struck sorrow, and all over Virginia and
the whole land. And when the good Markey Lafayette hears
of it there in France—he's gonna bust out crying and the
great tears go rolling down. (*The gun sounds on the river*

again.) Listen at that gun! All day it's been firing, firing to
honor him—and bringing the people together up there at the
mansion house—where my master lies stretched out and still.
Later now they're gonna fetch him down the hill there and
put him to sleep with Massa Lawrence and the others—when
we get the tomb ready. Boom it goes and boom again. And
the hills and the woods rattle with the sound of it and everything grows still, grows still and grieving. (*He looks up at
the sky and stares around. He shakes his head.*) Seems like
everything done turnt dark since it happened. Yeh, like that
time the sun 'clipsed and all the chickens started to roost in
the middle of the day, and the cows lowed like at evening
time for milking. (*He leans once more on his rake.*) I knowed
it was gonna happen—the way he kept working hisself to
death—all time working for the people and trying to get
the nation started. I was with him through it all—yes, sir,
through it all—from the days when I was a young sprout out
there in the Ohio country where I got my leg broke and up
to now. I would say to him, "General, Mr. President, Suh,
Your Excellency," I'd say—"Go to the devil, Billy," he'd
say, and I'd keep right on, "You got to quit it, you got to
rest. You's strong as two oxes and a bear-cat rolled into one
—but you can't do everything all by yourself." "Not much
time left, Billy," he'd say. "I got to keep working." And he
would look at me and smile that smile of his'n and say better
to wear out than to rust out like Mr. Franklin tells. (*His
voice breaks and he wipes the arm of his old coat across his
eyes.*) Sometimes he'd get loose from one of them big jobs
he had to do for the country, get loose and we'd come back
to Mt. Vernon. "Billy," he'd say to me, "roll up our sleeves
now—we're gonna do some farming." "Real farming, suh?"
I'd say. "Real farming, Billy—none of this mommicking.
We're going to make things hum." But no sir, hardly would
us get things to rolling again and the field hands and the slaves

to working and singing about "happy is the morning"—the
land getting green and fat again—no sooner done than here
they'd come—Mr. Mason, Mr. Randolph and Mr. Madison—
and up north they'd send out a cry—Mr. Franklin and Mr.
Hamilton and Mr. Adams—all calling on the General. Things
is in a mess again they'd say and you got to come help fix
them. And that's the way it was—no rest day nor night—
till it killed him off. Ah, there goes that gun again on the river
—boom-boom. (*He starts on, his rake in his hand, his lament
rising*—)

> "Then grieve, grieve, grieve,
> For death's a hard trial."

American Theme—The
Common Glory

The Common Glory is designed to tell in entertainment form the story of Jefferson and his immediate associates and their fight to establish a new government in the new world. The play aims to make realistic and immediate in emotional impact something of their tragic difficulties and near-failure and to celebrate some of the hard-won fruits of that fight.

In days of crisis and confusion we look back on our early builders with the superiority of a hindsense, a knowledge of accomplishment already done which tends to obliterate most of their blunderings and confusions. Tested by time, the experiments of our founding fathers, their groping utterances now appear pat and sure, marked and weighed. And their causes and effects are recorded and sealed away on dry library shelves—books most often written by even dryer experts and historians. We forget the human failures of these former men, the pain and the uncertainty through which they slowly shaped out a declaration of principles. We of the volatile and lively present are wont to accept without question the steadfastness of Washington and the penetration and almost clairvoyance of the minds of Jefferson and Lincoln. And the hard commonsense of Franklin has long ago taken on for us the mystic charm and authority of oracular and definite utterance.

We forget that the intent of the founding fathers and the strength of their creativity were generated out of a terrible insecurity. They had to choose a course of action for which they had no guide in the pages of history—no guide exactly. For every situation contained its unique problem. These men had behind them no pattern to copy. They only had their hard-won and experimental wisdom to illumine their way.

II

Thomas Jefferson was the foremost spokesman for the 18th century American political philosophy. He believed that good government was a compact or contract entered in upon by the responsible individuals mutually concerned in the enterprise. The method of progress and procedure was for him through the expressed will of the majority. But the privilege of majority rule carried with it the bounden duty of protection of safeguard of the minority. For out of the minority too the truth and progress might come.

Basic and integral elements of Jefferson's vision and philosophy, as everybody knows or should know, were freedom of speech, of thought, of education, of opportunity, of religion and the right of revolution.

The key to Jeffersonian philosophy and consequently to American idealism lies, I think, in the concept of the individual as a unit of absolute and prime value in himself. He precedes the group, he continues beyond the group. The group is but a quantitative accumulation of individuals. Jeffersonian democracy and the American political idealism are identical therefore with Christian psychology and ethics.

There is abroad in the world today a contrary view, a view which considers the individual—you, me, every person —as having ultimate and final value only insofar as he exhibits the traits and workings and fulfillments of the group. It holds that the individual is created and has value only by way of the group.

In our philosophy, the group has value and reality only by way of and in terms of the individual.

We might say perhaps that the American way of life takes its actual beginning in the loneliness of adult consciousness, in the singularity of the act of awareness of personal maturity and responsibility. The totalitarian way takes its beginning in a concept of togetherness, of mass shibboleths and rulings and pronunciamentos. The one is a way of life which comes into action because of the creative work of individual thinking which has preceded and produced it. The other finds its urge and practice by way of authority handed down by the edicts of group statement and so-called pragmatic metaphysics and precedes and precludes creative thinking—except that of the first authority. The one is of the person, the other of the institution. The one is first concerned with thought, emotion, ethical content. The other is primarily concerned with form, behavior, and methodology of the state. Both naturally claim to be concerned with the welfare of the people and are—the one conceiving the total welfare as an addition of single individual instances, the other conceiving the total welfare as that of a group movement or procedure in which individualism is absorbed.

III

I believe in the American way. I believe that the Federal system of states created here, if extended into a brotherhood of nations, would bring immeasurable benefits to the world, to the individual souls in that world. And what other souls are there in existence?

I do not believe that the totalitarian view of life, the view of authority, of dictatorship, of the all-powerful nature of the state and the unimportant nature of the single individual, is the true way forward for political man.

Now if the totalitarian method, the method of authority, of dictatorship, of knee-bending and unself-reliant souls, outrages something basic in the dignity of man's personality—and I believe it does—then in due time it is bound to fail. Free men will not wear the yoke of crass obedience indefinitely. The fact has been proved too often in history to be doubted, and the present political power extending its tyranny in Europe and Asia will ultimately dissipate itself and fall into counter-revolution. But it might be well to remember that the power of Rome lasted for more than 400 years. And that fact should and does give us concern.

IV

But however grave the concern, I for one do not believe in the necessity of brutal war. If we have learned anything from wars it is that they never settle any real problem of man—they only settle the lives of countless young and innocent dead. War is no way to settle differences in philosophy. A difference in fists does not settle a difference in brains. Matters of the human spirit are not subject to final appraisals and definitions in terms of physical facts.

We have a great truth in our political philosophy here in America. But it is handicapped, not flourishing freely and untrammeled. Let us help this truth to free itself so that it may prevail.

It is high time we began to clean our own house, to get rid of our injustices, straighten ourselves up. We need to look about us and weed out the evils that have begun to infest the temple of our devotion. These evils meet us everywhere we turn. Like tares in the night they have grown up through our lethargy, our carelessness, our selfishness as keepers in the master's vineyard. Let us be up and doing. Our democratic way of life now needs regenerating and revitalizing among us. It is a matter of religion and service to that religion.

v

For our nation is only as strong as the ideals of the citizens in it. Jefferson knew this, he taught this. In our schools we learned the fact. But day by day, year by year, we have continued to breed and grow diseased and deformed citizens—in the slums in our cities, in the Negro section in Chicago, in the dark loathsome dens in Harlem, in the rotten shacks throughout the South, and in the blasé apartments of many a glittering metropolitan Park Avenue. And even today we are breeding misguided little school girls and boys by the millions, all to a paean of advertising praise for a materialistic and gadget way of salvation and life which contradicts the very idealism and spiritual values we claim for the vital and triumphant democracy of our nation.

The cynical neglect with which we of the 20th century have treated our heritage has now at last boomeranged upon us. For instance our failure in the single particular of entering into democratic world citizenship has created in that world a counter power which has risen to challenge us. But this challenge actually challenges only our weaknesses and our abuses. It is time they were challenged from the outside. We long ago should have destroyed them from the inside.

So at last the time has come, the hour is here. We can now busy ourselves with cleaning up our declining way of life, making it strong, recapturing and building and filling out into actual practice the vision that Jefferson and the founding fathers had for us—a vision which was only partial in their case but as pure as it was partial. They gave us something to go on. And we have not measured up to it. We have not contributed our share in its continued growth. But the time has come when we must.

Closer to Broadway

I was revising my play for the summer rehearsal. Looking up, I saw Mary Elizabeth standing in the door.

"Well, for goodness sake," I exclaimed.

"Yes, it's me," she said.

"Come in, sit down and tell me the news."

"There's not much to tell. I thought I'd come by and say hello and see how everything looked from last year."

"We are sure going to miss you. I was sorry to hear you couldn't come back."

"Oh, believe me, I wanted to come back—but I—well—I thought I'd better try something else."

"I know. What are you doing this summer?"

"I'm working with a group up in Connecticut. It's closer to New York."

"Yes."

"And do they pay you well—better than we did, of course?"

"It's not much pay. Yes, even less. But then I'm—I'm—"

"Closer to New York."

"Yes, that's it. I knew you'd understand."

"I hope I do—a little. We've got some New York actors with us here this season. They've been very close to Broadway for several years."

"I know how you feel about that. But in the fall I'm hoping to get a chance. Another girl and I are going to get a little apartment and try our luck."

"But of course you know that New York is full of good actors—thousands of them—and eighty per cent of them are unemployed."

She looked at me with a calm untroubled smile. "I know that too," she said, "but there's always that twenty per cent, and I'm hoping to be one of them."

"And how will you support yourself while you're trying to break into this lucky twenty per cent?"

"I've saved a little from my teaching this winter. And father and mother are going to help out."

"That's fine of them. And you're lucky to have parents that can afford it."

"I'm afraid they really can't. Father works in a department store. But then they're proud of me. And I simply can't let them down."

"Well, remember next summer we'll hope to have you back."

"Thank you," she said.

She went away.

II

I was casting my play for the new summer's production. I looked up and Mary Elizabeth stood in the door.

"Well, for goodness sake," I exclaimed again.

"Yes, it's me," she said once more.

"Come in. Sit down and tell me the news."

"There's not much to tell," she said.

"I didn't hear from you. I thought maybe you would write."

"Yes, I should have, perhaps, but then I was always on the go so much. Your letter of introduction helped."

"I'm glad to hear that."

"I got in to see all sorts of managers. Then I had wonderful luck and got a chance to study under Jethro Marcus."

"And how did you like Jethro's method?"

"Wonderful. And then I studied under Simeon."

"And did you finally get a part?"

"I got a part—a small one of course, a bit—in *The Wild Unicorn*."

"I don't remember—"

"Of course. It didn't open. But I had an Equity contract."

"Too bad," I said.

"Oh, but Broadway is so exciting—so exciting." And she dabbed her little cotton handkerchief nervously to her lips.

"And you're not discouraged?"

"Oh, no. No!"

"And you'll be going back in the fall when the season opens?"

She shook her head. "I'm afraid I won't," she said.

"Good for you," I said heartily and unthinkingly.

She looked at me with a restless, troubled smile. "I know how you feel about Broadway," she said.

"The real question," I replied, "is how Broadway feels about you. How about working in our show this summer? Last year we had a good season—made some money."

"Oh, I'd love to, I'd love to, but—"

"It wouldn't hurt your professional standing," I said a little sharply.

"Please," she said.

"You can understand my natural irritation," I spoke up. "I've talked to hundreds of girls like you. You remember I warned you—eighty per cent, I told you."

"And twenty per cent, I answered back," she said mirthlessly. And then she went on. "I'm going to get married—that's why I'm not going back."

"Fine," I said.

"It's Walter, the boy back home. We grew up together. He loves the theatre too—in a way, he does."

She held out her hand. "Goodby," she said.

"Goodby."

III

I was rehearsing my play for the third season's production. I looked up and Mary Elizabeth stood in the door.

"Well, for goodness sakes," I said, "just like old times."

"Yes, it's me," she said.

"Come in and sit down and tell me all the news."

"I thought I'd come by and say hello and see how everything looked from the last time I was here," she said. "I'm married now, you know."

"That's fine," I said. "You told me you were going to be. And so it's farewell to the theatre."

"Oh, no," she said. "Walter and I are working some in a little theatre group in our town. In fact, we founded it."

"That's the stuff," I spoke up heartily. "That's where the young people need to spend their talents. At home. If we can get our young people doing this sort of thing throughout the country—"

"I know," she laughed. "You could talk for hours on the subject."

"I can," I said stoutly. Then she looked out the door and called. "Walter, come in here." A young, well set-up fellow came in and was introduced.

Mary Elizabeth looked at me with smiling, joyous eyes.

She beckoned to me. "Come along—you." I followed her and her husband out to their car.

"There," she said. I looked in the car and on the back seat in a basket was a gurgling, healthy baby.

"It's our best production," Walter spoke up.

"Well, that's wonderful," I said. "He looks like both of you."

"Oh, be shamed of yourself! It's a girl. Can't you tell?" she said.

"Not at this distance," I answered.

"You ought to. It's so obvious—her face, her hair, her teeny little hands."

"Yes, yes," I said.

"And you know what she's going to be when she grows up?" she asked.

"No, I don't."

And the two answered in unison, "An actress!"

"Yes," said Mary Elizabeth, "we've already decided to make an actress out of her, a great actress. She'll be on Broadway some of these days. You wait and see."

"I'll wait," I said.

Custodians of Greatness

Out of the belief in the individual and the works of his brains and hands has come a new age to the world—the machine age. The inventive genius of a free America has led the way for its coming—with the turbine, the steamboat, the cotton-gin, the telegraph, the telephone, the electric light, the development of the dynamo and combustion engine, and more lately the automobile, the airplane, the radio, the motion picture, television, the atom bomb, and many another marvel never allowed for in heaven above or earth below.

Seventy-five per cent of the machine age inventions have come out of America. And all of them, some more and some less, have carried with them the potentialities of greatness of service, enlightenment and inspiration to all men everywhere. For it is the nature of the machine to be universal in its humility of servitude, its obedience to a master's will and hand. A carburetor works for a Chinese or a Japanese, an air drill cuts for a white man or a Negro. The only requirement is the knowledge of how to run them. And that knowledge is not a matter of color or creed or race or birth. It is a matter of opportunity and diligence.

Now of all the machines which man has created for his own betterment and self-expression, none it seems to me for the present is loaded with greater possibilities than the motion picture. Here is an invention which is unlimited in its power for progress and good—for entertainment of the finest sort, for inspiration, glory, grandeur, whatever term you wish to use in interpreting human nature's ideals, its vagaries and vanities. There is nothing like it and never has been before—not the radio, phonograph, newspaper, hardly books even—for its impact and the shaping of people's lives, their thinking, manners, education, customs and their deeds.

For here is a universal and democratic instrument for humanity's using—a story-telling medium with power to match any requirement and need of any creative mind. Nothing that can be imagined or thought or glimpsed or dreamed is beyond its ability somehow to state dramatically and excitingly. The hopes and fears and ambitions and disappointments and griefs, the varying faiths, the tuggings and despairs that fill our lives from the cradle to the grave are material for its recording and its telling. The all-hearing ear, the all-seeing eye of the sensitive modern camera have made it possible.

And today the movies have a part to play greater than ever before—a part in the order and welfare of the world's future. The jostling nations and races and creeds of this frantic planet are striving to get closer together in spirit and thinking as they have got closer bodily and physically through the use of that winged engine the airplane, and the radio. And no agency is better fitted to help bring this to pass than the motion picture. For the screen appeals primarily to the eye and can hurdle language barriers more easily than the written or spoken word. It can reach directly to an audience whether in Moscow, London, or Berlin with the illustrated story it has to tell.

But the movies are not fulfilling their potential greatness. They are stopped and stymied by the producers and the manipulating moneymakers. These traitors and betrayers of the common weal and the people's heritage have with their cynical and scandalous exploitation of the human weaknesses flooded the world with sensationalism, melodrama, novelty, glitter, froth, shine and stuff for sensual appetites. They have continued to portray our country as a land of excesses, of easy money, of poverty and crime, of gangsters and tough guys, of dull and ignorant politicians, of furred and empty-pated women, of cheap success, of hokum heroism, of easy sex, wastefulness, bad manners and adolescent intelligence.

The only honest exceptions I know are the pictures of Walt Disney and Charlie Chaplin.

A group of South American business men, artists and journalists of many nationalities were recently visiting the United States. They were surprised at what they saw. "Your country is not at all what we expected," I heard them say. "We had only known it through your movies. How different it is! You are an intelligent people, kind, generous. You read books, like music, have writers, painters, singers, statesmen, leaders, theatres, teachers, scientists. You have a great culture. Truly, it is not all money and trading and profit-taking with you. We had not known it before."

And so it has gone.

Well, the war has changed many things, and there is hope even in this. And it would seem that the time has come for us to release this powerful instrument of human expression from its enslavement and let it begin to show the true heart and nature of this land of ours—something of its real inner dynamic soul and idealism which you and I know it to have and which is at one with the true heart of men everywhere.

Tragedy—Playwright to Professor

You speak again of "the Aristotelian glass darkly." I will try to be as frank. This ipse dixit authority continues still to hold our minds in thrall. And it would seem that the time has come when it should no longer do so—what with our modern experience in relativity, bio-chemistry, Bergsonian elan vital and atomic power. By any test of "process" and "growth" the formalism of the great Stagirite ought now to be weakening its grip.

You speak too about the protagonist Gilchrist in the folk-play *The Field God* which I wrote many years ago. You are right—I did finally end the play with the traditional and vengeful Jehovah having the last word. And why shouldn't he? Why should we always keep looking for indications of an inevitable and triumphant moral order and justice in tragedy? In certain tragedies—I almost said "kinds of"—yes, and in others maybe not.

Why do you maintain that in tragedy a man's failure and death must always seem to be just—right, necessary?

Thus you say our hearts are wrung.

It may be their very injustice that wrings our hearts.

The protagonist Gilchrist had certain values which he had grown up to believe in. And his struggle to save those values was simply his struggle to save what he counted most real in himself and to himself. When he fails in this struggle and loses these values, then there is nothing much worth living for. So it seems to him, and he had no sense of need to try to make it seem otherwise.

You suggest a different sort of ending for the play—the dogged continuation of his existence. Let him leave his house, you say, and go out to tend his farm in desperation and loneliness. This to me would be too much of the "strip of life" kind of thing.

No, rather let him kill himself in disgust at his environment and in his own proud self-pride. Let him refuse to accept the final insult of bowing his will before a selfish and unjust God in whom he would not, could not believe. So his suicide is his one defence against hypocrisy, even his own.

You ask about the ending of another play of mine—*The House of Connelly*. I had originally intended a tragic conclusion. It was cued out of life. Patsy Tate, the young heroine in that play, represents the creative process of life and the brave optimism of youth for a new day. In the tragic ending she was set upon at the gay proud moment of her existence (her wedding night) and murdered by two old ignorant and jealous household Negro servants—goddesses of the Southern hearth, protectors of the old way of life and enemies to the new. So Patsy Tate represented the fresh young South destroyed by the old. And there are plenty of particular instances below the Mason and Dixon line where this sort of thing has occurred and keeps on occurring.

But I decided against this cruel pathos ending. I chose another. This optimistic ending was likewise cued out of life. For often here in my land new ways have taken hold and produced new and better conditions. There is now obvious everywhere a young and vibrant South, creative and fresh and on its way to mighty doings. So that was the kind of ending I chose, and I let Patsy Tate live. And in her living she

showed her mettle as mistress over the household and its re-
bellious servants.

It may be that a great deal of your perplexity over such
matters as these comes from applying the Aristotelian logic
of the content to that of the form, or vice versa. We have
inherited a certain formal theory already made up about the
nature of drama, and we test the examples we meet by it. I
suspect such testing. You mention the word "pessimistic."
That is an example of what I mean. Isn't it important to consider only the struggle that the characters wage in their fight
to make their lives and their purposes prevail. Let them win
or let them go down—the struggle is the important thing.
How can you decide on pessimism by way of the ending
only.

You quote Hegel at me. I remember somewhere that philosopher does say, "a character which is dramatic plucks for
himself the fruit of his own deeds." Again it is yes and no.
For often a dramatic character has to eat the bitter fruit someone else has planted for him and someone else has plucked
likewise. And always there is Jesus Christ and the suffering
Buddha and lately Mahatma Gandhi, and any and all of the
martyred saints down history's past. What of them? I mention them to match your phrase "the tragic flaw." May not
this tragic flaw you exhort often turn out to be the lack of
any tragic flaw—whereby the character is thus put out of
joint with the times which have their flaw? The jut of his
more perfect personality, say, may fail to fit into the warp
and curve of the environment of error around him. And so
against the power of this error, this surd, this wrinkle or
fault in an overpowering and antagonistic universe, the protagonist wrecks himself and perishes.

You ask what is the nature of the dramatic struggle. I
would say that any character who is awry with any or all
of his three worlds—himself, his neighbor, the outside uni-

verse—is the subject matter for drama if he struggles to dissipate this awryness. There must be struggle, you know, human struggle, and wherever that occurs there is drama. If the struggler fails or pays too big a price for what he gains we have what we call tragedy. If he wins without too great a struggle we have less tragedy, and so on. If the struggle is one of seem-so and therefore incongruous, we have comedy.

And of course here we are always talking about tragedy as an art, about comedy as an art.

In all tragedy, whether classical, romantic, naturalistic, realistic, expressionistic—to use the scholar's empty terms—the problem of evil, of sin, raises its head. And that means good, virtue, raises its head also—in fact has already raised its head first.

Some say that dramatic tragedy is essentially a depiction of the struggle between a right and a wrong, between truth and untruth, between good and evil. This may be a sound theory, but to understand and agree to it I would first have to qualify it. I would say—very well, provided we understand the nature of the wrong, the untruth, and the evil—how they got to be that way. It doesn't seem as necessary to understand how right, truth, and good got to be their way. We accept them a priori and instantly in their own right. Such is the nature we are born with.

Hegel's theory, as everybody knows, is different from this. The highest tragedy, he says, is never a struggle between good and evil, right and wrong, but between two goods, two rights. His illustration is as you will remember, *Antigone*. Antigone was caught in the dilemma of a contradiction between her devotion to her family and her loyalty to the state. To adhere to one she had to deny the other. Both loyalties were right and yet they were in contradiction. For love of her family she buries the accursed body of her traitor brother. The state takes its revenge and destroys her. But the state in the person of Creon pays likewise a fearful penalty. His own son, betrothed to Antigone, hangs himself in grief, and his wife dies for the son. Too late Creon relents, and peace is restored. Justice is calm again. But what of the poor destroyed ones?

Well, I leave you to your own judgment as to his theory.

You speak about a definition of drama. How do you define it? I will hazard a definition, a simple one—Drama is a story acted out.

To paraphrase Hegel again—Drama in its best sense is the presentation of human actions, human relations and aspirations in their actually visible form to the sensuous and imaginative consciousness. It is exhibited in spoken speech, in behavior, in the pantomime and habiliments of living persons— (This includes of course the simulacrum of puppetry.)—who in this way give expression to their intents, their hopes and dynamic will—the plunging forward, the moving on, the realization of the concern of their selves. The dramatic action then depends on conditions of collision, human passions and character, leading to actions and reactions which in their turn call for further resolutions of conflicts and disruptions until finally the high point of tension and explosiveness is reached and the storm is over and the curtain falls.

I will try another definition—Drama then is the representation of will working toward its fulfillment.

And now we come again to your statement about the "unhappy ending." What do you mean by an unhappy ending? Better to ask perhaps why grief and sorrow, suffering and pain depicted on a stage give happiness to the spectator—if the drama is a good one. Yes, why do people in a theatre take pleasure in the spectacle of unhappiness. Why?

We all know Aristotle's answer which seems to me only half-right—namely, we are purged by pity and fear with a seasoning of terror, and this purging, this catharsis, gives us relief. It sounds as if he is talking about a constipated soul. What do you think the Christian answer is? Or the Buddhist, or the Hindu? Wherein does a religious aesthetic differ from Aristotle's classic and pagan one? You see, I am asking you a lot of questions now. I wrote something about it elsewhere and I will restate it here.

Now in regard to the cruel, the disgusting, the fearful, and other such kindred subjects, why is art pleasing which deals with them? The answer is that in the treatment their "ugliness" disappears and they become sublimated and idealized with the emotion and intent of the artist who interpreted them. We view them as representatives of actuality and not as actuality itself. And the emotions and ideas aroused in us by the contemplation of these examples of art fill us and increase the abundance of our personality and are therefore pleasurable.

To repeat—how is it possible to get pleasure out of witnessing or reading a tragedy? The answer seems simple, and is simple. For the spectator or reader is stirred to sympathy and pity for the tragic sufferer *in whom he has grown interested*, and a feeling of benevolence is aroused in him. And therefore the quality of mercy is doubly blessed.

The joy of sympathizing, of feeling self-sacrifice, of giving out of our heart unto another is pleasurable, pleasurable to the deeper and more spiritual self and is only unpleasurable to the shallower, more physical, less spiritual self.

The urge to associate with, to help the suffering one, to lift him up, to ease him, brings with it not only the feeling but often the very picture or pictures of the completed association, and therefore a gained fullness of personality in this giving out results. Accordingly the feeling is pleasurable.

In tragedy, then, man's benevolent and unselfish self is called more strongly into play than not. And in giving, potentially and imaginatively (and never actually or factually) he the spectator the more completes himself therein and within. For such giving is born of love.

For love gives and hate takes away. Tragedy, then, arouses love. And the pleasure resulting therefrom is not a selfish or fearsome one at all—as Aristotle would seem to have us believe. In fact, the purgation or purifying he speaks of comes, and I think can only come, through this very unselfishness of giving, this love that loves to give.

II

You talk about the types of dramatic tragedy—and about the highest, the less good and the worst. I wish you would give me some examples. I happen to think that the word "type" is a sort of empty word. For instance, would you place Macbeth ahead of Agamemnon or would you set the Book of Job over Hamlet or Hamlet over Ezekiel? Or Dante and Milton over Isaiah?

And another subject I hope you will discuss more thoroughly—the protagonist himself. A lot of questions occur to me. Can we have pity and fear and brotherly in-feeling for the essentially evil without being evil ourselves? What about Milton's Satan?

Perhaps you will say that the true protagonist must be truly human—human enough like us other poor mortals to excite in us a fellow-feeling—he with his fumbling and failings, his tragic flaw. Here we have once more raised up the question of sin and error and punishment for the same.

But are sinners and faulted souls the only protagonists for tragedy? What about innocent ones? Can't innocence be truly tragic? Perhaps you will say no. I rather think you will. Then I ask can ignorance be tragic? And now we come upon another mystery—what about knowledge and experience of evil which are guiltless—knowing sin without sinning? Mystery to me. Maybe the answer lies in the imagination, a somewhat detached and platonic one which is not besmirched by the vibrations and tremolos of evil, but nevertheless feels and knows.

I keep going back and wondering too whether you are right in your iteration that there must always be this certain justness, a matter of receiving one's deserts in a true tragedy —at least from some sound point of view or other. I won't contend the point that Macbeth deserved the fate which fell upon him. Suppose, though, he had won his wild intent, made his purpose prevail, how would we, the spectator, the reader, feel about him? It is the same sort of question we might ask perhaps about Hitler with his Lebensraum and gas chambers of extinction.

No doubt you could say that only in the fact that Macbeth and Hitler received the deaths they deserved because of the crimes they had committed in their fell and fearfully purposed ambition—only because they received their deaths could we accept them as tragic human beings. But maybe that is not enough to say. Would they have to have some good in them or else not be tragic? And mustn't they suffer the passions and terrors, the strainings and uncertainties of their course as they proceed?

All right then, to move on, let me say that a totally evil man is not properly tragic. Then again what about a totally innocent one? Does he stir in us tragic emotions if some undeserved fate falls upon him? Perhaps you will say that his case is piteous, like a child accidentally killed by a car, or a bird struck by lightning—not truly tragic.

What about Jesus Christ? Like Zacharias when I am treed, I always turn to Jesus. Does his story excite in you this feeling of pity and fear, this sympathy, this yearning, this desire to help?

Obviously there are many kinds of dramatic tragedy—perhaps as many kinds as there are specimens of it. Maybe there is no type, but only specific instances, and what we call type is merely a similarity between groups or numbers of these instances.

Macbeth is a kind of tragedy. *Hamlet* is another kind. *Oedipus* is still another and *Antigone* still another. All kinds are specific and individualistic. And I doubt there is any type among them except insofar as we arbitrarily and uncritically say so.

I am reminded here of an oriental philosopher who said, "There is only one way into the world, but an infinite number of ways out of it—birth is one, but death is infinitely varied." And he also said, "Through the blue depths of the sky the bird flies, but the tips of its wings are never stained in it, and it is written that with faith a man thinks—faithless he cannot think—and he who worships God as the great king milks heaven and drinks it day by day—his food is never exhausted."

Yes, I believe a tragedy can be written about a totally evil man, either beginning as such, or ending as such. Here I would define evil as the self-ruined individual. There can be tragedy of the evil-good man too, the weak and volatile. There can be tragedy of the perfect man. There can be tragedy written about the struggle of evil against evil and tragedy written about the struggle of good against good—and so on through all the wordage combinations.

And the power of the production would be determined by the skill of the artist, by his ethical intuition and his poetic fervor.

Shakespeare has always seemed to me to lack the ultimate kind of greatness—that is, a religious intuition of life. Where Aeschylus lacks some of Shakespeare's human warmth, the tender particularity, the rich foliage of existence—there is in him nevertheless a sense, an awareness of man as an ethical creature, a soul caught in the dilemma of right and wrong which satisfies me better than Shakespeare's miraculous power as a sensory and romantic writer.

For me the highest subject matter of tragic drama then is the struggle of man to reach, to discover, the self within him as an abiding reality. And that reality will the more be discovered in him by his struggle to make the right prevail —to oppose evil.

I think that this reality is the true Fountain of life's youth, the Source, the Logos, the Tao, the Way, the Secret—propelling itself ever outward in waves of life, mystic, germinal, creative in its being.

When the effort toward self-realization is so fierce and strenuous as to destroy the self—in the very terms of goodness, the very principle of righteousness which the protagonist labors to reach or establish—then here is basically to hand the richest and realest dramatic material of all.

And don't claim me a pragmatist in the William James sense—not entirely. Each and everything is more than what it is used for. There is a recalcitrancy, an objectivity and self-sturdiness there, which is the essence of each individual person or thing. But I agree I am a pragmatist in the Alfred Whitehead sense, or even in terms of Plotinus, and of Thomas Aquinas and Aristotle insofar as he, the latter, accepts his forms and what he calls his "types" as coming created out of an ideal of reality which actually is reality. This is that Tao, Logos, that germinal essence spoken of above.

And I do not believe in the academic imaginary concept known as "a body of truth." But I do believe in truth as a creative process which the protagonists of our great dramas can create and sustain. And I believe also that the importance of these protagonists lies mainly in such creativity and such sustaining.

In this then they are free men. Tragedy deals with free men—or men seeking to be free, or with slaves struggling to break their bonds, or of free men passing in spite of all activity into slavery. Their greatness in each case depending upon the struggle they wage against their enslaving fate or destiny or chance—call it what you will.

And your final query— Is the universe maleficent or beneficent? Or is it neither—simply neutral? I would prefer to say it is neutral though always potentially either of the other two. It is simply there to be used. But since it has existence in its own self and existence in its own way, man must learn the nature of that way, the way of nature, and work with her according to her needs and rules or he will be wrecked. And then in his sorrow he may cry out that she is hateful and evil —and that cry would likely then be more pathetic than tragic—but just the same it might wring our hearts and make us weep.

Body and Soul

We human beings can do so little about our physical body. As the Bible says, can we by thinking add one cubit to our stature! We are born predestined as to our anatomy. We are of such a semblance, formation, physiognomy, coloring and physical bent. This body, this solid flesh, is not of our doing.

Some power, some creative desire, some over and out-pouring hunger that fulfilled itself in the melting embrace—this gave our body its birth even as it in turn in the dithyramb of fulfillment will procreate and give birth to other bodies.

This creature, the body which we feed and massage and bathe and perfume and comb and curry, remains selfishly and adamantly what it is. It carries its own license with it, its own routine waywardness and ritual of self-behaving. The heart beats on whether we sleep or wake, the food digests whether we sit or run, and the cells of our flesh grow and wax relentlessly old. One's shoulders are so broad, one's legs so long. One's head and bust and hips such a shape and size.

Thus we can only palp and preen and brush the sensitive skin and feathers of this our physical brother—with the power of course to make him sick and maim him or keep him tuned up and in health's glow.

But these are pretty and outward matters. He is his own man.

But in our spiritual, our psychic selves, we are our own

man too. The man of the self, of creative possibilities. How strange and yet how just this twin set-up! The spirit is free and makes its own law. The body is beholden to the law of slavish cause and effect, the determinism of nature.

We cannot make our bodies then as specimens of our own handiwork. The biological process of nature in the main does that. But we can make ourselves what we should be as creatures of intelligence, of religious aspirations, of imaginative reach and daring—and the requirement is never that we be more than we can be. We can be free and morally responsible, filled with eternal and immortal thoughts, able to set up the shining dramatic symbol of everlasting life fast in the middle of the gates of death!

Eternal life beyond the grave!

Out of the anguish of body and soul, out of the certainty of oblivion and total disaster, man, the intelligent one, man the dreamer, man the spirit, builds the opposite. Out of death he makes a vision of continuity. Out of evil he transmutes good. Out of necessity he envisages freedom. Out of temporal causation—immortal consequences.

Physically then, and of the animal earthly kingdom, man is doomed to live a little while, then die forever. But intellectually, imaginatively, spiritually, he is spaceless, timeless, supernal and immortal—even as he thinks so.

Now materialistic science declares for the law of the conservation of energy and the eternal existence of molecules, atoms, electrons that make up our bodies. But there is no such immortality. Each atom as well as the whole vast physical universe could vanish, cease to be in the blinking of an eye—and will. The truest values lie in the other realm. And in that realm, man can be as great, as real, as generous, as ideal, as loving, as true, as aspiring and as accomplishing as he wills himself to be, and as his own spiritual imperative demands. And it is not a matter of size but intensity.

The thing that counts most then is that man is his own spiritual creator and master.

As to his body then, the individual concerned is helpless to do anything significant about such a fact and detail. Nor is it important for him to do too much about it—since he can't.

But to repeat once more, as for his spirit, his moral nature, his thinking, his *soul*—he can do everything about *them*. He can become a better man, a more evil man, kinder, less kind, lazy, energetic, accomplishing, and so on.

And the purpose of this inner man, this spirit, insofar as the body is concerned, is to see that the body is kept in co-operation with the intent and opportunity of the spirit.

And the intent and opportunity of this spirit in regard to its own self is that it grow in charity—its own charity.

Man Creative

Man is a spirit charged with knowledge and the responsibility of that knowledge. He lives in a kind of mortal immortality different from the immortal mortality of the animal. His kingdom stretches far beyond that of nature's blind vitality into the radiance of another world.

Call this extension of man's spirit, this separation and aloofness from the animal, this cleavage between two kinds of living, a matter of difference in degree only as the scientists since Darwin are wont to do, yet the difference is there. We see it in man's outward creativity.

We intuitively know and feel it within.

From the moment when as a growing child we pass from our animal and instinctive babyhood into the miracle of our rational and thinking humanhood, we live as reasoning and responsible beings, conscious of our beginnings and our end upon this earth, conscious of non-existence, of all-encompassing death about us. And because we are men and so consider as men, we the more strive to endow our deeds with the effort of permanence, of immortality against death's dissolution, degradation and decay.

In the reach of our soul's visioning we become the rebel against omnivorous, all-devouring time. With the power of deliberation, of choice and deciding, no matter how we got them, we work, use, shape, control this time to our purpose, seeking to fill it with eternal and fadeless images and expressions of ourselves.

We build institutions, set up monuments of the most lasting material possible, write books, dramas, dream dreams and embody them forth in immortal thoughts, thoughts of immortality.

As a creative spirit man is always a pioneer into new ways and methods of believing, acting, and thinking—ways never allowed for in the blind stress of matter and the seething of nature's laws and commingling forms. He is a maker of new forms, a manipulator of this same recalcitrant matter, a legislator and adjudicator of a new law. And his way is forward out of the grip of the old animal law of death and darkness into a newer one of life and light.

Nor does he bother too much with the darkness behind from whence he came, as he the seeker and the see-er climbs up his hard path, however toilfully, that leads to selfhood's mastery. In the words of the poet he has loved the stars too long to be fearful of the night, or to bother with the sheeted ghosts of its despair.

Man and man only has the possibility and the powers of endowing the animal nature in himself with the glory nature never had and never thought to have. This it is that sets him apart from all things and beings else, whether living or dead.

II

Men can live like animals if they will, even like clods of earth if they so desire. This is true not only of individuals but of whole masses of people. And being each a soul's worth and full of potential and ideal accomplishments, the larger and more inclusive the mass the more wasteful and degrading such living seems to become. But wherever man is found at his best and finest he lives not as an animal but as a man—an immortal soul.

And the path waits straight before him, the shining goal forever beckoning bright ahead.

Then why does he so often fail to travel in it, to see it? What is the hindrance, the handicap to his attaining his haven and his home? What estops him, when he would reach the rainbow wonder of the soul at journey's end? How account for his too frequent tragic failure in his quest?

Why do falling, cruel wars come on him when his heart pleads peace?

In his efforts to create and make actual his dreams and noble enterprises man time and time again runs afoul of his fellows who likewise are bent on the same purpose of creating and building—whether on the same level of intent or not. This is his tragedy, the tragedy of man against man, human purpose against human purpose, and not the tragedy of man against nature.

For in nature there is no tragedy. She is neutral forevermore, neither for nor against, neither malign nor beneficent. She is only available—either to inspiration or frustration or not.

But why do men so run afoul of one another? Why this contradiction between them, this head-on collision of climbing souls?

Well, is not man still swaddled and swathed in trailing clouds of ignorance and fear that blind him? Does he not glimpse the light, the true path only dimly, mistily? He does not see it steadily and clear, does he? Thus, as Bacon says, he mistakes signs and symbols for what they are not, mirages for reality, the meaning of specific things for other and general things.

Often the better will appear the worse to him, or the worse the better. A too narrow loyalty may grip him now, a confusion of preachers and leaders frustrate him there, a blinding emotion or upswirling passion, planted and bred from ancient deeds and circumstance, flood through him in a crisis of decision and scatter his plans to foolishness.

So tricky a thing is the heritage that brought him here.

Or it may be allegiance to family, or institution, or nation, or convention or custom, compelling his denial of a larger and more universal allegiance, involving him in a binary one-sidedness. Ambition may pull against honesty, love against honor, will against authority, pride against humility, even the spirit against the flesh—numberless the hazards and pitfalls that lie along the path of his endeavor, countless the strains and tensions that tend to divide him in himself.

And it could not be otherwise, for this is the living nature of man's being—organic, growing, developing, and separate and distinct from the unquerying and integrated animal.

But the endeavor is there. The effort ever to build himself a better and more perfect life continues in spite of all odds against him, and often psychologically because of these very odds.

There is a primal impulse, an impetus, in man toward the creation of a truly beautiful and noble world. And however obscured, hindered, detoured or misused it may be, this primal impulse still stirs in his heart, lives in his soul as a fiery spark, ready to burst into a divine and burning flame.

Or if it is not so, then all is lost.

The Mind's Freedom—A Case in Point

I have been an ardent believer in democracy all my life. And I expect to continue to be. The principles upon which the government of this nation is founded seem to me basic and right. My admiration for the founding fathers is as fervent as it is unabating.

I believe in individualism, in the fair competition of talent and initiative for the prizes of life to be won. I believe in free enterprise and the philosophy of hard work and thrift and upstanding responsibility.

The totalitarian and authoritarian philosophy of government is contrary to the character and spirit of the American way of life. It shocks our nervous fibre as a nation. Ours is a doctrine and a practice of freedom. But this does not mean license of behavior and free proclivity and appetite in every form.

With us liberty means responsibility. Our liberty is gauged in terms of our responsibility. And our responsibility is accepted in terms of our freedom. The one is the inalienable concomitant of the other and should always be.

The early pioneers who perished on Roanoke Island; the mothers and little children who were swallowed up by the thousands in the merciless onrush of terror, plague and disease at old Jamestown; the persistent, the unyielding, the tenacious and idealistic Pilgrims who fought for and held a precarious and gradually strengthening foothold on the harsh shores of New England—these and their everlasting spirit of sacrifice I believe in, and I believe likewise in the men who followed them—Washington, Jefferson, Franklin, Adams, the first American martyr John Rolfe, and that timeless other martyr Abraham Lincoln.

Out of their struggle and endurance and suffering came these certain principles then—freedom of religion, freedom of speech, of thought, of assembly, respect for the person and soul and rights of others, freedom of education, of the right to search for and find the truth—the truth unhindered and unbound.

Now a university by its nature is dedicated to these principles—to the discovery and teaching of truth. In this the institution is like the thinker, the artist, the dramatist. All that exists, all things, all natural phenomena, all ideals and histories and arts and cultures and handicrafts and artisan creations and the deeds of men—these are the object and material to be used by the inquiring mind.

To the seeker of truth no door of research is barred, no segment or arc of the great circle of surrounding ignorance is to be marked off as forbidden to attack. Truth is free. The true seeker must be free to find it and to use it freely and to thus push back the frontiers of prejudice and fear that always wait their chance to engulf us.

The free and active mind is the one certain and sure defence against an ever-threatening barbarism. When this goes down the citadel of glory falls and the funeral pall of omnipotent death eclipses the guiding light.

The teachers and scholars of our universities are in a

special sense the keepers of this light. And as such they must have free play for their intelligence and imagination. How else can they be worthy of the calling they follow? How else can they honestly train the young minds entrusted to their care and pass on to them their principles and conclusions and axioms of fact fairly arrived at?

Neither by reason nor stretch of logic can it be maintained that a university should take unto itself the duties and rights belonging to the state itself. When an educational institution sets up a law of its own demanding of its prospective teachers an affidavit or statement as to the kind of thinking and beliefs and politics they hold, then it is infringing on the realm and the rights not only of the individuals concerned but of the government itself.

For if holding "a foreign political faith" is a crime or misdemeanor, let the state or federal law say so and take action accordingly. It is not the business of a university to preempt the state's prerogative. It is not now, nor has it ever been.

The university is an educational institution. It is not a political imperium. Nor is it a police power.

If totalitarian philosophy is at variance with the true doctrine of democracy, and I believe it is whether of communism or fascism, then the means the university has to combat it with—is not by fiat or decree but by a more zealous devotion to and spreading of the truth. The one way to fight bad ideas is not by passing bad laws, but by producing better ideas.

Matters of preference and taste and belief and all the vague and shadowy splendor of the mind should be and must of necessity be free. They cannot be controlled by statutes, decrees, personnel sheets nor institutional and administrative ukases whatsoever.

II

The tradition of freedom of conscience and individual rights has long been established among us. It is embedded in the very heart of English liberty and the American dream, and for generations it has been.

Out of the past comes many a voice saying so, and in the air around us today we hear them speaking.

Jefferson writing to his nephew at the College of William and Mary in 1787 said, "On the other hand shake off all the fears and servile prejudices under which weak minds are servilely crouched. Fix reason firmly in her seat, and call to her tribunal every fact, every opinion. Question with boldness even the existence of a God; because, if there be one, he must more approve of the homage of reason, than that of blindfolded fear."

John Stuart Mill, the English philosopher, writing in 1859 declared that the spirit of liberty "comprises first the inward domain of consciousness; demanding liberty of conscience in the most comprehensive sense; liberty of thought and feeling; absolute freedom of opinion and sentiment on all subjects, practical or speculative, scientific, moral or theological."

And Charles W. Eliot, in his inaugural address at Harvard in 1869 said that "A university must be indigenous, it must be rich; but above all it must be free. The winnowing breeze of freedom must blow through all its chambers."

Oliver Wendell Holmes in one of his famous decisions in 1919 declared "That the best test of truth is the power of the thought to get itself accepted in the competition in the market."

And in vetoing the 1919 Lusk Laws requiring licensing for schools and oaths for teachers, Governor Alfred E. Smith wrote—"The profound sanity of the American people has been demonstrated in many a crisis, and I for one do not believe that governmental dictation of what may and may not be taught is necessary to achieve a continuance of the patriotism of our citizenship and its loyal support of the government and its institutions."

Charles Evans Hughes, in a letter to Speaker Sweet of the New York legislature in 1920 said, "If public officers or private citizens have any evidence that any individual or group of individuals are plotting revolution and seeking by violent measures to change our government, let the evidence be laid before the proper authorities and swift action be taken for the protection of the community."

A. N. Whitehead, philosopher and mathematician, in his address on the future of Harvard said some years ago, "But the ideal of the good life, which is civilization—the ideal of a university—is the discovery, the understanding, and the exposition of the possible harmony of diverse things, involving and exciting every mode of human experience. Thus it is the peculiar function of a university to be an agent of unification."

Dean Wilbur J. Bender, in the March, 1949, issue of the Harvard Bulletin wrote—"I know of no faster way of producing communists than by making martyrs out of the handful of communists we now have. Forbidding them to speak would be not only treason to the ancient traditions of Harvard and America, it would be proof that we have something to hide, that we have lost faith in our principles and in our way of life."

And Dwight D. Eisenhower, in his installation address as President of Columbia University, more recently said— "Who among us can doubt the choice of future Americans, as between statism and freedom, if the truth concerning each be constantly held before their eyes? But if we, as adults, attempt to hide from the young the facts in this world strug-

gle, not only will we be making a futile attempt to establish
an intellectual iron curtain, but we will arouse the lively
suspicion that statism possesses virtues whose persuasive effect we fear."

Again and again thus have we seen men stand and speak
as witnesses to the democratic way of life and the freedom
it brings.

III

For nearly a hundred and sixty years the University of
North Carolina at Chapel Hill has had no loyalty oaths and
tests for its professors. The teachers naturally have been
expected to be competent, decent and law-abiding men. If
they did not prove to be so, they soon found themselves moving on.

The compelling power of ideas, of public morality and
general opinion have been sufficient controlling forces for
our university, and in fact they have given it much of
its inner dynamics and motive strength during the past
years.

Now suddenly, as part of the rash of narrow nationalism
and fear which have broken out, the professors at this same
university are confronted with something our forefathers
did not deem necessary—something in fact which the very
charter of this university admonishes against—namely, the
setting up of a test of political faith as a prerequisite to teaching.

In the act of 1789 establishing the University of North
Carolina, Section VIII says that the trustees shall have power
"to make all such laws and regulations for the government
of the university and preservation of order and good morals
therein as are usually made in such seminaries and as to them
may appear necessary; provided the same are not contrary

to the unalienable liberty of a citizen or to the laws of the state."

Time without number our courts have ruled that man's thinking, and imagination, his ideals and soul are his own—which is only confirming a precedent fact. The Revolutionary War our forefathers fought and won for us had to do with this identical question. Long ago our Declaration of Independence and our Constitution declared the same in their advocacy of freedom of faith, freedom of religion.

For generations it has been understood that laws and statutes and promises and affidavits and rules and regulations have no legitimacy and strength against these principles. To repeat—matters of the mind live in a realm of their own, the realm of freedom.

Only when thinking and faith and beliefs pass into action and behavior can they be dealt with by legal power and authoritarian control. And always through due process of law this is to be done.

IV

The emotionalism now spreading over the American political front is understandable enough. These hysterical whirlwinds of fear and prejudice are always stirred up by the vast suction of the train of Armageddon when it goes by. They are the resultant of the fierce feelings, whether of loyalty or hate, which war generates and leaves turmoiling behind.

This being true then, we should be the more mindful not to be swept off our base. Let us continue solid and strong in our ancient faith. Let us hold fast to the principles of our national being. These temporary attitudes and fixations will pass. In time they will pass. And the heritage of our long-tried democracy will remain once more unsullied and affirmed above them.

Out of the past the great organ voice, too, of John Milton speaking—speaking for ages ahead of him: "We should be wary therefore what persecutions we raise against the living labors of public men, how we spill that seasoned life of man preserved and stored up in books; since we see a kind of homicide may be thus committed, a kind of massacre, whereof the execution ends not in the slaying of an elemental life, but strikes at that ethereal antithesis, the breath of reason itself, slays an immortality rather than a life."

And as for books, so for the quickened and sensitive genius of the scholars and teachers who write them. Let us not massacre that!

The University of North Carolina has gone astray in its requirement of loyalty oaths for its teachers. Let it amend its error at once and thereby return to the noble tradition of liberalism and freedom it has enjoyed so long.

Playwright to Politician

My former appeal to you some weeks ago to help do something about the atom bomb and the growing and awful crisis in human affairs was motivated by as honest a feeling as the one that motivates you in your affirmed devotion to the Constitution of the United States and the denial of the idea of one-world government.

But as a citizen and a dramatist I must keep on pleading the case that if we are to escape the degradation and wastage of another awful and tragic war—even a greater one in madness than that not so long ago ended—we must do so through the coordinated intelligence and dynamic good will of our leaders—among whom you by virtue of your position, are important.

We the people cannot save ourselves.

For our political guidance and salvation, or not, we have through democratic processes elected such representatives as you to speak and act for us.

It is both futile and cynical then for these same spokesmen to turn back to us, the people, and say—as you have so often said in your campaigns and as the president himself said in his recent Columbus, Ohio, speech: "It is up to you"—the "you" in this case being as in all like cases of evasion of responsibility, we the people.

The plea I put to you, Senator, is the same plea the citizens everywhere in the still-free world are putting to their leaders and representatives: Give us a leadership, provide us a program, a way forward, a righteous course of action for humanity, humanity safe and sound, unified in purpose—a true world unity.

I ask you to speak out there in the halls of our Congress, where brave and fearless men now and then have said their say. Stand up and speak for the right.

We need a religion. That is the word. We need to be taught to feel our democracy as a religion. You are the leader. Teach us. Democracy as a religion has never yet seized upon you. Why not?

We need to be fired to an idealism worthy of our wants, our wishes and our needs. You cannot trade us into it. You cannot swap us or buy our way toward that shining goal. Nor can you back us into it by fearful terror. We all must work, get out and work, suffer for it, prove ourselves—we must earn it.

We must have a chance for devotion to our ideal. Help to give us that chance. You are there in Washington. You are near the source of political knowledge. You are part of a great political power. I am not and can never be except in my own small way of suffrage as a citizen.

You say, "Our position grows more desperate and the more that is conceded to the totalitarian powers, the more is demanded." Do you mean then that our program as a nation is to be one based upon the will and wishes of another nation? Are we to adopt the policy of no concession, of getting our bristles up, of firmness or whatever you want to call it and nothing more? This, is only negative. For it is defensive. Negativity has never built a great people, a great nation. It never will.

This is the girding-up-of-loins time spoken of in the Bible.

The good will which we still bear the world must some- how extend our democratic theory forth and reach the sensibilities of that world. Our theory must become a practice. The feeling of brotherhood which we as a people want to adhere to—we, the leaderless people want—must somehow be made known to that world. Our military leaders by virtue of their calling and interests cannot be the bearers, the apostles of this message.

These military men cannot help us. Our civil leaders like you, I repeat, must.

And I tell you, our virtues will not of themselves soak under oceans and over arid plains and across arctic wastes by some automatic and economic process of osmosis and affect and reach the hearts of men. They must be preached and practiced, they must have their muscled and striding witnesses and workers.

And so I continue to cry the United Nations at you—you who have been sniping at it, you who have been summoning off its personnel for trials by water, fire and venom. I cry at you one-world unity full of hopes and accomplishments. And you fling a national constitution back at me and no more. Will you continue to work for a world divided and help to confer upon us the final gift of universal death?

This is a spiritual matter. And only from the spirit can the answer come.

There is possible a greater constitution than the one you have sworn fealty to. There is possible a world federal system under which could be subsumed the fierce and violent nationalism which you illustrate.

How can you continue to deny that a program of world sovereignty which would take precedence over national sovereignty, which would include national sovereignty dynamically in itself, how can you continue to claim that such a program for action is stupid and impossible?

The sum of meaning of the New Testament which you claim to know and love so well, the New Testament which you have taught in Sunday School these many years—is built upon this truth of cooperation, upon the gesture of the friendly outreached hand and not the balled-up inimical fist.

How can I fail to look upon such a leader with suspicion when he piously announces one program on Sunday in the church and for the rest of the week in the halls of Congress denounces the very ideals of universality which he has so dogmatically claimed.

I am not such a fool of course as not to realize the necessity of time and tact, the powerfulness of the appropriate hour, the diplomatic move. The rule of Jesus Christ, the philosophy of the New Testament, in national or international affairs, cannot be immediately put into practice. And if it could, it would not likely bring us off victors over the Russians or anybody else. No.

We would be swallowed up as saps and suckers.

But still an ideal is expressed there which we can cling to and visualize and which by hard service and work help to bring to final if slow realization.

And I am not fool enough either to continue to believe—as you seem to believe—that we will somehow reach international accord and cooperation by repeated mutual acts of suspicion, mutual distrust and displays of power.

All squeal and no wool, as the Devil said when he sheared his hogs!

I see nothing wrong that our moral reach should exceed our practical grasp. Was this not true in 1918 when for awhile we held the moral leadership of the world?

I keep declaring for the same simple truth, the obvious truth, that as men act honorably one with another as individuals, so must the nations strive to do or we shall continue to live maimed and mutilated and perishing and maybe —as it most lately seems—not live at all.

We of all nations on earth seem best fitted both by theory

and former practice to lead the way in allaying suspicions and hates and terrors of other nations and of taking pioneer action in this particular—world unity.

Let us.

South America and Asia still believe in our good will toward them. I am sure they do. They know the principles on which our nation was founded. They are acquainted with the dynamic of our heritage. They know of Washington, of Jefferson, of Madison, of John Adams, of Benjamin Franklin. They know of Abraham Lincoln, of Woodrow Wilson and his dream of a united world.

They believe that our hearts are basically just and sound. I think they do in spite of the surprised and helpless dead in Hiroshima and Nagasaki. But this belief has grown weaker of recent years and months. We must somehow make stronger proof of that good will, make it live vital and strong again. This is the real balance of power to work for. And we can do it if we are determined to.

You have studied your Bible, as I say. You know. You know that action is religion, that religion is character, character is destiny, both for the individual and for the nation. Highflown words, but they are true. You know what we as a nation, as a people should do, must do if we are to survive and our children are to inherit from us the sort of world they have a right to inherit.

Then help us.

Make your choice, and make it right. Choose, and as you choose the right and the truth, the people will follow you and follow with devotion and enthusiasm. Save us.

For we the people cannot save ourselves!

The Mystical Bernard Shaw

I

Some years ago I spent an evening with George Bernard Shaw. He was then at the height of his powers, and his barbs and gibes and penetrations of thinking impressed me so vividly that I went home and wrote down the things he said.

The world perhaps no longer takes this eloquent and wonderful man as seriously as once it did. His philosophy of social reform, his crusading for noble causes have lost something of their following in these later years. Nor does his satirical and political pamphleteering seem as fresh and virile now as it used to do, or as chock-full of clever puns and cracks and doggerel blackguarding, whimsy and performance. But that may be our fault too.

I like to think of the Shaw of my interview. He had something to say in those days which needed saying. And in the light of the present tendencies and antagonisms and technological trends loose in the world, I think what he said then has even more point now.

I was in London at that time studying the theatre on a Guggenheim Fellowship, and a friend of mine mentioned to St. John Ervine, the English playwright, that I would like to meet Bernard Shaw. Ervine kindly said he would try to arrange it. A week or so later I received a postal card from Mr. Shaw saying he would be glad to see me briefly on the following Thursday evening at seven.

That Thursday afternoon I went out to a Charlie Chaplin movie. And when I came out of the theatre later a terrible rainstorm had risen. It was one of those turmoiling Dickens nights to be endured only by way of a good book and a warm snug fire. I finally found a taxi and arrived at the wrong address owing to a confusion of street names. Arriving at what I hoped would be the correct address, I accosted a policeman standing dry and authoritative under an awning near by.

"I'm trying to find Mr. Bernard Shaw. He's supposed to live here at 4 Whitehall Court."

"Shaw, Shaw, you say?"

"Yes, Bernard Shaw."

"Hmm—I don't—"

"Oh yes, but you do—George Bernard Shaw, the dramatist, the writer, the public speaker. His picture was in yesterday's paper. He made a big speech in town. You know—Bernard Shaw."

But the bobby shook his head, staring at me. "Sorry," he said, "I never heard of him."

I entered the carpeted hall of the apartment house and, after the usual preliminaries with the desk clerk, I took the elevator to Mr. Shaw's floor. When I stepped out, I was met by a rather plump, elderly lady.

"I'm Mrs. Shaw," she said, extending her hand. "I'll show you into Mr. Shaw's study. Like you, he's been caught out in the storm. He hasn't come in yet."

She took me down the hall and into a huge salon or room which didn't seem at all like a study. A big gas log burner or something red hot was going in the fireplace.

"You can dry yourself here," she said, then smiled and left the room.

I stood by the fire and studied the room—the thick carpet, beautiful furniture, the lovely books, the flowers, the numerous photographs—the last testifying with their autographs to the esteem in which the famous playwright was held. Prominent among these were the faces of Mrs. Patrick Campbell and of Professor Albert Einstein.

In a moment there was a swift padding footfall down the hall. The door opened and Shaw came in. He was bareheaded and his white brush of beard was sparkling with rain drops. His cheeks above were fresh and rosy as autumn apples and his eyes bright and clear. He was tall and thin, or seemed to me so, and was dressed in a tweed coat, dark woolish shirt and tie, checked knickers and stout walking shoes.

"Good evening, good evening," he said cheerily, and his whole lean form breathed a gusty outdoorness. He stuck a long pinkish hand toward me. "So you were out in the weather, too."

"Yes, sir," I said. "I am very late."

"Not at all, not at all." He chuckled, and with a quick animal-like step was at the hearth. Here he reached his hands out to the fire, rubbed them briskly together, turned around several times, smacked his lips and champed his beard up and down. Yes, he was an old boy, all right, a young old man, a sort of satyr or gnome. Such was the immediate impression he made on me. He started to sit down, then sprang up.

"This place is chilly," he said, "too large, too chilly. Come, let's go into my workshop." He led me into a sort of den, a snug, cozy little room stacked with books to the ceiling. A small gas range was going, and in front of it was a heavy table piled with papers, manuscripts, letters, and the odds and ends of a busy writing man's life.

"Sit down," he said. He sat down, also, arched his fingers together and rested his elbows on his long thighs. "Ah, this is nice, this is nice." He said it several times. Then he rubbed his hands vigorously toward the fire, wiggled himself, and flew suddenly up again out of his chair.

"Let me show you the view." He opened a door onto a little balcony. "See the Thames below," and he pointed to the rippling light-twinkling water of the river. The rain was whooshing down, but he didn't seem to mind.

"It's a real Dickens night," I spoke up, raising my coat collar against the drenching flood.

"Heh," he laughed, "Dickens didn't know anything about modern London."

The remark made no sense. And before the evening was over he spouted forth a lot of other remarks the point of which I couldn't see. Part of the time he would seem to be jeering, gibing, talking nonsense. Then again he would screw up his lips, cock his domed straight-backed head to one side, peer at the gas flame and talk levelly and seriously for a moment. But only for a moment. For then chuckles would break out of his beard, he would wag and nod his head, wiggle his ever-moving hands in the air, and be off again on some tangent of furious peppering conversation.

II

When we had closed the door on the falling rain and sat again in front of the flames, he looked over and asked me what brought me to London. I told him something about the Guggenheim Foundation and the fellowships which were awarded to scholars, students, playwrights, musicians and artists to go abroad and study in the fields of their interest, and something about my interest in the people's theatre.

"Yes," he said gleefully, "these millionaires are always doing silly things. There's nothing they won't try to buy."

I made no reply to this and none was needed, for he followed on with a volley of words. "Tell me about the American theatre. The Theatre Guild—they've done some of my things; wretchedly, no doubt. Have you any people of promise over there?" (He pronounced "there" much like the extreme folk pronunciation in the South—"thar.")

I started to tell him something about our playwrights, but he interrupted, waving his hands as he went on. "I suppose it's skyscrapers and money, money and skyscrapers. I see no proof to the contrary. Yes, everything has its place, even when it's out of place." Then he peered through me, as if speaking in the empty air, and I was reminded of a statement I had just read in Stanislavski's *My Life in Art*, where he writes of Anton Rubinstein, the musician. "Unlike us earthly beings, he was not ashamed to look at people as if they were things," Stanislavski said. "I noticed the same habit in other great men whom I met: for instance, in Leo Tolstoi."

Finally I got a word in edgewise to say that America was proud of Eugene O'Neill. It seemed that in him at last we had a real dramatist.

"Yes, O'Neill," he chattered. "A man of some talent. Yes."

"Have you seen any of his plays, Mr. Shaw?"

"No, I haven't. I've read one though. Someone sent me a copy of—let me see—*Strange Interlude*. Maybe O'Neill sent it or the Theatre Guild. I read it."

"Did you like it?"

"I was asked that same question. Who was it? Maybe Arnold Bennett. I told him that after reading *Strange Interlude* I was sure *Back to Methuselah* was only half long enough."

And then he was off in a great scurry of devilish snickering. When he had quieted himself he said, "Plays are never too long, if they are really good. That's what I meant about

Strange Interlude. It's not too long. It's only not good
enough. A great many critics have called me long-winded,
which is to say they find my plays dull and dispirited, empty.
But we must remember that they are the critics and they,
because of their calling, have already been ruined and don't
know what they like or even what they should be looking
for. Who does know? you say. I'll tell you—the people.
These same people you mentioned—they know. They're
not always able to say that they know in so many words,
but give them a chance and by their presence or absence
they will tell you.

"I remember when we were rehearsing *Man and Super-
man* the actors, the Devil and Don Juan, came to me in despair
—and remember actors are as notoriously empty-pated as the
critics—the actors came to me, saying their speeches were
so dreadfully long that the people in the theatre would walk
out on them—something that had never happened in their
long and illustrious careers. So I had it out with them hammer
and tongs. But I was right. I knew I was right. The people
would listen because there was something said in those
speeches. I didn't give in. Finally they did. I was right. The
people, to use your American phrase, 'ate it up.'

"I once held an outdoor crowd for seven hours. So far as
I knew, I never lost a man. In fact I kept adding to the flock
of listeners, strollers kept coming in and—staying in. You're
from the southern United States, you say?"

"Yes, sir." I was now getting accustomed to his abrupt
changes of mood and subject matter.

"An interesting region—with your politicians and lynch-
ings—a place of great talking and fulminations—to what
purpose I don't know." And he threw back his head and
laughed his soft "ho-ho" like an ungainly boyish Santa Claus.
"Incidentally, how is my old friend, Archibald Henderson
in Chapel Hill?"

"He's fine," I said.

"He's a remarkable fellow. Quite remarkable."

"He is that," I said. "I live across the street from him and see him often. He's one of the outstanding men at our university."

"Really?" His great white beard quivered and the pair of bright bird-like blue eyes peered across at me. "Why?"

"Well, consider his books on the drama, his biography of you, sir—" I was fighting back a little now—"his knowledge of mathematics, philosophy, English literature, history—he's written volumes in all these fields."

"Yes, and he informs me he's now writing a study on theoretical physics. He'd best let it alone."

"Why?" I asked.

"Because that sort of science is a pitfall. Yes, a pitfall, a quagmire into which naive and unsuspecting souls wander and disappear like the innocent dumb animals that sank forever into the pitch lakes of prehistoric time."

III

Then, in a tirade and flood of words, he began an attack on modern science. I sat and listened as he cracked and whipped his way on. He went back to the beginning of the world in his survey, then came up through the Mediterranean and Phoenician folklore ages. He skippingly sketched the artistic period of Greece, the early church age, Constantine, Julian the Apostate, and on into the Middle Ages, with the Crusade and the Revival of Learning, the Arabian scholars, the Song of Roland and next the Italian Renaissance with Dante and Petrarch thrown in for good measure. Then he swiftly rattled through the Elizabethan age, the Restoration and on to the advent of Darwin.

"And in all this long stretch of time man exhibited a wonderful freshness and vigor of the human mind," he said, "which exemplified itself in amazing works of art, works of literature and folk songs and sagas. But after Darwin, and in the main because of Darwin, a blight began to come over the world. The religious leaders, the scholars, the dreamers, the poets, the seers became more and more infected by the scientific virus, and scales covered their eyes, so to speak, scales which cover them to this day."

"You don't believe in modern science then?" I ventured, as he paused for second wind.

"Not at all, not at all," he chirped. "They write me down in their books and say I do; say I too am one of these half-mad folks, one of these modern cranks myself, with all sorts of plans and ideals for a scientific socialistic state and the methodical betterment of the common man. Of course I'm for betterment, improvement. Who isn't? But progress has nothing to do with the modern scientific views. In fact, modern science hinders progress. Understand what I mean?"

"No, sir, I don't."

"No, the younger people everywhere don't understand it, for they too have been blinded by their teachers in this scientific age. I myself am a devout mystic. The critics, the biographers, have never discovered it. And why not, when it is the first thing they should have discovered? Because they too have lost the power of seeing truly. They are Pharisees, their ritual has ruined them, has blinded them to all simple elemental truths. If a thing is not obscure to them it's not important. All men are by first nature mystics. Now modern science denies this mysticism, and in such denying goes counter to the deepest nature of man. It blasphemes man."

"I see," I said.

"You are an apt pupil then," he jeered lightly, "or perhaps it is the teacher." And he threw back his high gnomish head and laughed "ho-ho" again.

"There are only two great principles in man—his mystic nature and his common sense. And when in his theories or his practices he deviates too far from either, he wanders in confusion and darkness and is lost. That is the condition of the modern world—confusion and darkness. Blinding science affects every phase and calling of man's present endeavor. It is a blight in the field of art, in the field of practical affairs, in religion, in politics, economics, everywhere. And it all began, at least it all got channeled toward its present degradation and despair, with Darwin.

"Take our current scientific philosophers like Eddington, Jeans, Whitehead, Bertrand Russell—they well represent what I mean. They go round and about and cry out in their articles, pamphlets and books with a great splurge of nonsense. And all their researching and pother come to one thing only—an enervating pessimism. Just recently I was re-reading Russell's *A Free Man's Worship*, and if there's anything free in what he had to say I couldn't find it. Rather he made out a poor case for ruined and forlorn man. To Russell we are a sort of insect doomed to certain disaster and death on a blind and wandering planet. Yes, with these fellows all beneficence, all rightness, all that men once lived by through the ages has been destroyed. For an enriching mysticism and guiding common sense they have substituted these strange diabolical things known as instruments and recordings, statistics and measurements—the telescope, the microscope, the test tube and the X. The X sounds a trifle encouraging."

Here he shook himself, leaned forward toward the gas flame and rubbed his now rosy hands sharply and slitheringly together. "Yes, I think I see the beginning of the passing of this age. And I think, I hope, we shall soon begin to come out of this eclipse into sunlight again."

"How, Mr. Shaw?"

"I don't know how," he answered. "But I do know that

mankind in its deepest feelings and urges won't suffer denial and frustration indefinitely. For nearly a hundred years now it has been trying to live and draw sustenance from a blind and misguided dogma, the dogma of science. Perhaps Einstein marks the beginning of a new age, or at least the ending of the old." I waited and he went plunging on. "For Einstein, no matter what his theories and formulae may look like to the scientific priesthood, is a disciple of mysticism and common sense. He is mystical in his acceptance of a principle of activity, of energy which is everlasting and self-continuing, and he believes in the common sense appearance of things, of things being what they appear to be."

"But the fourth-dimensional world he talks about could hardly be called the world of appearance, could it?" I asked. "It couldn't to me anyway."

"And yet what is the childhood world of poetry and faerie, of things as they seem, but this same fourth dimension?" he hurried on. "It is all a matter of how one relates oneself to the thing seen—actually how he sees it. That is the true relativity.

"Yes, life at heart is miraculous. The quicker we realize that, the quicker we release the wellspring of inspiration and vision and feeling. In a world of time and space this mystical principle expresses itself in things, in deeds, in objects, in symbols, and tokens if you will. Now, what are these things, these symbols and these tokens, these deeds? Are they something which the scientific explorers probe into and define by way of their delicate and complicated instruments? Or are these things what they seem to be to the ordinary common sense intelligence? Over there is a tree, a fence, a bird. Is it a tree, a fence, a bird, as it appears to our sight, or is it something else, some collocation of energized molecules, atoms, electrons, protons, ions or whatever kind of "ons" the scientific quacks with their barbaric vocables wish to denote it? It is the former, of course."

IV

And then from gazing queryingly at the gas flame he jerked his head around and demanded with sharp directness, "How far do you consider the moon to be from the earth?"

"Well, sir, according to the figures—"

"Bother the figures! Speak frankly."

"It's supposed to be two hundred and forty thousand miles or thereabouts."

"Yes," and he spanked his knee, "supposed to be. Now you see what happens in your answer. When I asked you, you had to think, to recall, to make your reaction by way of some misguided astronomer's figures." I stared at him in astonishment. "Let me ask you this—how far does it seem to be?"

"Well, that depends, Mr. Shaw—"

"Yes, yes," he interrupted impatiently. "It depends—"

"No, I mean—well, when it's up in the middle of the sky it looks farther away than it does when it is near the earth, say just rising as a full moon in the east."

"I see, I see," he went on quickly. "Perhaps so. For a moment I thought you were beginning to enter the realm of the psychologists with their subjectivism and objectivism nonsense."

I broke into a little laugh to hide my dismay at all this twaddle. I lit a cigarette and emphatically offered him one, though I'd heard he neither smoked, drank nor ate meat. He as emphatically shook his head and hurried persistently on. "Then how far away does the moon appear to you to be—well, when it is at the full—just rising?"

"Mr. Shaw, I hadn't thought of it like that in terms of distance."

"Ah-hah, but that's just what the poet or child or artist does think. You've taken courses in astronomy, I suppose?"

"Yes, sir, in college—one."

"Let me tell you an incident." And he turned his chair around, facing close to me, his voice full of energy and almost petulant pleadingness as if driving home his point in my mind was the most important thing in the world to him.

"Some years ago Albert Einstein came to London to make an address here. I was on the committee to welcome him, in fact I was to introduce him to his audience. He was to arrive the night before the lecture. Being engaged, I asked Mrs. Shaw to meet him at the train and see him established in his hotel. I don't know what the occasion for my remissness was—perhaps I was busy on a new play, I don't recall. I had never met Mr. Einstein, though he and I had passed correspondence with each other for some while. Late at night of the day he arrived I decided to take a walk along the Thames there. It was a beautiful moonlit night and as I strolled along, the figure of another stroller overtook me and we walked somewhat side by side for a while.

" 'I see, my friend,' said the stranger presently, 'that you are enjoying the beauty of the night.'

" 'Yes, I am,' I replied. 'The moon is lovely.'

" 'And how far, my friend, do you consider the moon to be distant?'

" 'I should say about forty miles,' was my answer.

" 'Remarkable, remarkable,' said the stranger. 'To be exact, it is only thirty-seven-and-a-half miles away. My name is Einstein.'

" 'And mine is Bernard Shaw,' I said, and we shook hands. Yes, the great scientist was also a believer in common sense like myself. *Appearance is reality*. We both were willing to accept the testimony of our eyes."

And he broke into his "ho-ho" laughing again. And as he laughed, screwed up his eyes, and threw out his hands, I recalled having read somewhere that Mr. Einstein did not speak English. But there was no need to make mention of the fact. Now he was off again with his rush of language.

"So it is—a question of appearance and reality. Perhaps you know F. H. Bradley's book by that title."

"Yes, I do."

"Reality, the mysterious, the hidden, the miracle—appearance, a matter of common sense." With a wave of his hand, he chortled, "That's the sum of it. It is all basically a miracle. The expression of the miracle is the truth of the world of sense around us. These two are the common heritage of the people. And the scientists, the smart boys, the critics, the scholars, the experts, they believe neither in the miracle nor in the appearance of things. They are looking for something they call the fact and the law of the fact.

"Their knowledge has ruined them.

"When I was a boy back in Ireland," he went on, "I succeeded in getting a bicycle, in fact—notice I use the word figuratively—I think my mother purchased it for me. So off I set myself to ride. But I couldn't ride. Day after day, hour after hour, I tried the provoking thing. But I couldn't master it. The people along the street had great sport out of my trials and sufferings. They would come out on their porches, peep over the fences, through the fences, and watch me climb on and fall off. Finally from sheer shame I began to rise before dawn and try to break the thing in when no one was looking. But the neighbors soon got wise to that and rather than be robbed of their sport they were willing to be robbed of their sleep. So up they got, too, as early as I and waited for the moment when I would dislocate my neck. I made no progress at all. But I was a determined boy. Then one morning I got on the bicycle and suddenly rode. I've been riding since that day. How do you explain that?"

I made some answer about the final coordination of muscle

and mind. But he snorted. "Whoh! A matter of conditioning, eh?" he jeered. "So the experts would say, the child psychologists would declare. But I will tell you what it was—a miracle." And he broke into his exultant chuckling again and peered beyond me, as if I had suddenly become a post or an image of a thing which happened to be present at his soliloquy.

v

When he had stopped laughing and wiped the delirious tears from his eyes with a large snowy white handkerchief which he pulled from his lapel pocket with a fastidious flourish, he went on. "Consider my case as a writer. The critics of the world, especially the critics of America, don't know how to appraise my plays for the simple reason that they are looking for things in them that aren't there. And yet it's all as simple as a child's belief. And because my plays are so simple, these pseudo-wise fellows never know what to make of them. They consider me to be an apostle of cold reason, of argument, of dialectic, of sharpened wit. Nonsense, I am a child mystic, first and last. My dramas are filled with the child's point of view. These fellows should begin their interpretations of my works somewhat as follows: 'Mr. Shaw's plays begin where they end and end where they begin.'" He halted suddenly and stared at me, his mouth partly open and a teasing, whistling sound slipping through his hairy lips.

"I don't quite see," I said.

"You should see. It is all as simple as twice two. My plays are interludes, as it were, between two greater realities. And the meaning of them lies in what has preceded them and in what follows them. The beginning of one of my plays takes place exactly where an unwritten play ended. And the ending of my written play concludes where another play begins. It is the two unwritten plays they should consider in order to get light upon the one that lies between." He grew silent and observed the fire with suddenly heavy-lidded eyes. I felt I had overstayed my welcome, if that was the word, and rose to go.

"No, no, sit down," he said ruefully. "Or perhaps you have another engagement," and sheer disappointment was in his voice and face.

"No, sir."

"Then sit down. I want you to tell me about your country, especially about the movies. Have you had any experience in writing for the pictures?"

"No, sir, I haven't."

"It is a great medium and you Americans ought to feel proud of your creation—for it is mainly an American creation. Some of your producers have wanted to turn my plays into moving pictures. So far I have refused them, but in the meantime I have done quite a bit of study in the field and I am enthusiastic. I hope some day my works can be put on the screen. Now that the voice has been added to the pantomime, to the gesture, I think I may try it. I've already tried it in a small way. Have you seen the talkie I did recently?"

"No, sir, I haven't."

"That was fun, great fun. The boys came out to my country place, bringing a vanload of machinery. They set up their instruments and I performed before them. They said to me that I acted like an old hand in the business. 'Yes,' I said, 'for I've been studying the theory. I know all about it.' Let me show you."

And so he got up and there in his little den walked back and forth gesturing and cutting steps to show how he had behaved before the camera.

"At the first screening of the picture, I remember, I gave a little dinner. Gloria Swanson was there. 'Mr. Shaw,' she said, 'you would be a great movie actor if you cared to.' I was pleased naturally even if the compliment came from her. But of course I'm too old to try that now. But it's a great medium. Our writers ought to write for it. There's no power in the modern world like it, and it will become more and more powerful as it is more and more perfected. It's a pity that our moving picture actors and actresses have so little brains, and the producers less. But that will change too. And it will take more than a pretty face and figure some day to be successful in the movies, as I told Miss Swanson. She seemed to resent my saying so, but I didn't mind."

He leaned forward and rubbed and wrung his hands before the flame.

"In view of what you have just said about miracles, Mr. Shaw, I presume that *Saint Joan* perhaps is your favorite play."

"Hah, not at all," he said, jerking his head up and slinging himself back in his chair. "It has good things in it, but it's not my favorite play. My favorite is *Heartbreak House* and the reason for it is obvious. It has more of the miracle, more of the mystic belief in it than any of my others, and, too, it is a sort of national fable or a fable of nationalism. And being Irish, I ought to know. *Heartbreak House* is England. I meant it for England when I wrote it, before and during the war, and I regret to say I still mean it so. If the critics had the brains of a mad Tom they would realize it is my greatest play. But they don't. They all go following after the Maid of Orleans. Why? Well, because it's easier to follow, easier to follow where history says than to lead where life demands."

VI

I asked his opinion then about some of the contemporary dramatists writing for the English stage. He didn't seem to have a high opinion of any of them except Sean O'Casey.

"He is a man of genius," he said heartily, "yes, of genius. It's a pity he started writing so late. But then he has time to accomplish a great deal yet if he is careful of his health."

"I like him too," I said. "He is a poet in the theatre, and poets are rare."

"Yes, a poet," he affirmed with a nod of his head.

"Sometimes though, I think," I added, "that he lets his poetry outrun his dramatic sense."

"Do you really think so?"

"Yes. His speeches get to be too long. They go beyond the story point and are piled on for the sake of the language itself."

"And why shouldn't they be?" he snapped. "Let him talk, let the words pour out. Why be niggardly with speech? It's glorious. If he has something to say there's no reason why he shouldn't continue saying it page after page. Yes, it's all a question of whether he has something to say—something important, something interesting, something—yes, beautiful. I think he has. Shakespeare did it now and then and rather well at that, and look at Dickens, how rich, profuse, what a gorgeous spilling of language!"

"Yes, sir, but Dickens wasn't a playwright."

"It makes no difference," he declared vehemently. "Speech is speech, whether it occurs in a play or a novel. That's the great trouble, one of the great troubles with the modern playwrights. They cramp everything down. Every line must tell, every sentence must have some plot point, must hurry on toward the inevitable denouement, straight as an arrow in its flight. What's the result? Something dry and dead. There's an old saying about that. Consider the lilies of the field— that's it, that's what was meant. The flowers, the greenery, the luxuriant foliage of life. O'Casey has that. He's a man of genius, and I hope all good things for him. Have you seen any of his plays?"

"Yes, sir, I recently saw *The Silver Tassie*."

"That's a grand play. It deserves success, but critics think they have discovered something of what they call two different styles in him, poetic realism and a sort of Strindbergian expressionism. And so they've thrown up their hands in horror and written him down as a talkative Balaam's ass. They've pretty much killed the play already. Ah, these critics, these critics!" And he threw out his hands in apparently wild exasperation.

"I must confess," I spoke up, "that I thought the second act, the battle-front scenes, showed a rather abrupt change in style. I saw no good reason for such a break."

"And why shouldn't it change? The soldiers who had come from a peaceful environment back in Ireland where they talked in ordinary terms and had their day's business and quiet and calm to attend to, they themselves were in an abruptly changed environment there in No Man's Land. The cue is always from life, my friend, life itself. O'Casey was perfectly within his rights in writing the play as he did. The critics should have had sense to recognize his wisdom. But I suppose the play is dead now, dead for a while. There's nothing anyone can do about it. What other plays have you seen?"

"Yesterday I saw Robert Lorraine in Strindberg's *The Father*."

"Ah, what a bad and terrible piece! Strindberg was a great genius though, one of the greatest. But his sense of the miraculous was so overpowering that he failed as an artist to give adequate place to the ordinary world of common sense. There must be a balance, you know. So it was all rather bad, rather bad for him. For what he really had to say was crippled because of his exaggeration in one direction at the expense of the other."

He now rose suddenly, brushed himself off with his hands,

and I rose also. "No, no, sit down," he said. "We haven't finished talking yet. Perhaps you have a question or two you'd like to ask."

"Yes," I said, "I'd like to know if you are working on a new play."

"I'm always working at a new play, either a preface or the play itself or some defense for it even before the play is begun. I am living in a wild uncouth England, you know, and I have to put stockades around my dwelling. I've just finished a piece on the modern political millionaire, and I am thinking now of another play, the biggest thing I have attempted, one in which all the facilities of the theatre will be called on to their fullest. It's only an idea yet, an idea I've been thinking about and, in fact, an idea others have been thinking about. It has to do with this childish fanaticism about war—specifically with the Unknown Soldier." He stopped and gazed before him, his hands shoved deep in his pockets and that light, almost inaudible, whistle sounding through his lips again.

"Yes, sir—" and I waited.

"I've thought of using the combination of mysticism and science in this play, making use even of an actual miracle. There's to be a big scene when all the people are gathered on a certain night around the *Unknown Soldier's* tomb where the sacred and mysterious light is burning. Through some proper device and in the proper mood, this Unknown Soldier will rise from the grave. I've only thought about it in dim outlines. To the horror of those assembled, he proves to be not a soldier of their own country but one of the enemy who has been buried and honored by mistake."

He snapped his fingers and whirled around, and stood with his back to the fire. "I'm only considering it, you see. I haven't thought it out clearly." He stood silent for a moment and blinked at the rear wall. Now I rose again. This time he put out no hand to stop me, in fact seemed oblivious to my presence. I waited a moment and then told him I appreciated the honor of having met him and it had been a wonderful evening and so on.

"I've enjoyed it tremendously, tremendously," he said. "I trust you will come in again."

He followed me to the door and down the hall. And while we waited for the elevator he said, "If you have occasion to, please tell the critics back in America that the way to understand my plays is to realize, as I said, that they begin where they end and they end where they begin."

And with that he stuck out his long-fingered hand and shook mine energetically. I entered the elevator and the door closed. As it was descending, he rushed up and rapped frantically on the grille of the cage. The elevator stopped. "It's not a matter of how far away things are, but how close they are," he said. "That was my meaning in a nutshell. You see the point?"

"Yes, sir," I answered respectfully.

The elevator started again and the last glimpse I had of him was his standing there in the hall, staring through me and beyond with his fun-filled blue eyes.

Paul Claudel

For years I had admired the work of Paul Claudel—his poetry, his philosophical and religious writings and especially his plays. I had first heard of him when he was the French ambassador to the United States. And after the production of his beautiful morality-mystery drama by the Theatre Guild—*The Tidings Brought to Mary*—I read everything of his I could, his essays on the Orient, his interpretations of the Old Testament, his poetry and plays—*Joan of Arc, The Hostage, The Satin Slipper, Young Violaine* and others. And just lately I had read the correspondence between him and Andre Gide—two men at odds fighting fiercely for their individual views of life.

I was anxious to meet him.

I had come to Paris as a delegate to the UNESCO General Conference, and as soon as that was over I got in touch with Mr. Claudel, and asked him if I could visit him. He said he'd be glad to see me any time I could get down to where he lived in the south of France. So one day in July, I took the *Rapide* out of Paris and headed toward the Mediterranean.

It was late in the afternoon when I arrived at Lyons, and I hurried over at once to the bus station to get a ride across country to the little village of Morestel where Claudel lived. But the decrepit vehicle was already loaded down with people, baggage on top, bicycles, old valises, fishing tackle and farm utensils. It was a hot day, and the crowded faces protruding from the windows were wet with sweat.

The driver ignored my broken French supplications and finally flung himself into the seat, got the thing going and dashed away. I was left alone with my suitcase looking after it as it disappeared up the street in a swirl of dust.

I returned to the railroad station and got a hotel room nearby. Then I tried to phone the Claudels to explain I couldn't get a bus and couldn't get over till the next morning. But I found that the telephone was cut off from the Chateau de Brangues every afternoon at six o'clock, and M. Claudel could not be reached.

I took a taxi and drove up to see the old ruins of the amphitheatre above the town, but the watchman at the gate refused to let me in. The closing hour, he said, had passed—exactement!

At my hotel later when I was reading the paper I found that there was an entertainment up at the amphitheatre, a kind of outdoor dramatic music spectacle. I grabbed a cab and hurried up that way and spent a wonderful evening perched among the ruins of this ancient place, with nine thousand others, listening to Honegger's *Le Roi David* and Stravinsky's *Les Noces*.

The next morning I hired a taxi for six thousand francs and set out for Morestel and Chateau de Brangues. We drove and we drove and at last came to Paul Claudel's gray and ungainly chateau set back far from the road.

An attractive woman in her thirties came out to meet me, leading a little boy by the hand. The little boy was the very image of some of Claudel's earlier photographs which I had seen.

"Madame Claudel?" I began.

She smiled and said she wasn't Madame Claudel, she was M. Claudel's daughter, Madame Paris.

I was taken into the chateau—entering immediately without hall or vestibule into a sort of living room with a ceiling about thirty feet high, spotlessly clean and yet to a southerner, chilly and forbidding. M. Claudel was there and so was his wife—a delicate elderly flower sort of woman. There was also a young man who I learned was doing an article on Claudel.

We were introduced and soon got down to business. Claudel spoke English slowly. His daughter, Madame Paris, said she would stay and act as translator.

Claudel struck me as being a man very well preserved for his age—he being past eighty. His neck was very short, his head almost set down between his shoulders, and there was a sort of peasant sturdiness in his frame. I remembered that Andre Gide in his Journal had once described him as a sledgehammer man—*un marteau-pilon.*

"Do you mean you came all this way from Paris to see me?" he queried.

"Yes, I did."

"I appreciate the honor very much," and he bowed jerkily. I bowed.

"It is always a pleasure to meet an American, for you remember I have been much in your country," he said. "Yes, I have been there many times."

"We remember you with great—" I stumbled for a word —"great appreciation," I said, "as writer and statesman, sir."

"Merci beaucoup," he replied. "You said when you telephoned from Paris you wished to discuss some problems with me."

"Yes sir. I have read your books—your plays, poems and religious and philosophical writings, and you are the one man in France I wished to meet."

"Again, I am very much honored," he said, and he settled

himself deeply into his armchair. "But there are Sartre and the existentialists," and he dug his small stout fists into his thighs.

"But decadents for me," I said. He said nothing. "Have you time to spare me this morning?" I asked, casting a glance at the young man.

"Yes, indeed," he replied. "This gentleman and I have finished, and I have time. In a couple of hours we will expect M. Jean-Louis Barrault. He is coming down to talk with me about a new production."

"You are writing a new play then?" I spoke up brightly.

He shook his head. "No, not a new one, only the production of an old one. I shall never write another play. I am spending the rest of my life in religious writings. I hope to finish my book on Isaiah soon. That is absorbing all my attention at the present time. I mean—finish the second volume on Isaiah. I have already written the first."

"Yes, I have read that."

"Did you like it?"

"Yes, very much."

"Isaiah was a great spirit, he had a great vision. I suppose Isaiah is one of the most inspiring characters—inspiring for me—that the world has produced." He smiled. "You see, I am very much interested in religion."

"Yes," I said, "and that's what first attracted me to your work. Because there is such a strong religious strain in it. I—"

He raised his strong small hand. "True, true," he said, cutting me off. "Without religion the world will perish. That is one trouble with modern writing, I think. The writers don't have any religious convictions. This is especially true in your country." He smiled again. "You don't mind if I speak frankly about your country?"

"No, indeed," I said. "That is exactly what I wish you to do—that's why I came to see you, to hear you speak as you will on anything you will."

"I have written many hard things about your country," he went on, "but I believe the soul of the United States is a good soul. But, pardon me, I believe that it is an ignorant soul. I was only twenty years old when I first went to the United States. And being young and excitable, I spoke my mind freely about things I didn't like. Of course since those early days I have learned to know your country better and like her better. And because I like your country I feel that I will be more easily pardoned when I criticize it."

"Yes, yes," I said.

"I have spent much time in the Orient too, and of course the Orient is full of religion—full of religious consciousness, whether it is mixed with superstition or not."

"I expect to go to the Orient in September," I said.

"You will have an interesting journey. What countries will you visit?"

"I hope to visit Japan, The Philippines, Indonesia, Malaya, Thailand, Burma, India, Pakistan—and so on back through Europe home."

"Wonderful, wonderful. The trip must be very expensive."

"In this case the expenses are being borne by one of the educational foundations."

"Ah, those foundations," he said. "Money, money, money. Still, some of it is well spent, no doubt—the millions and millions they give away. In your case, I hope it is a good investment."

"I hope so too."

"I abhor most of the religion of the Orient," he said loudly. "Buddhism is terrible—terrible for what it does to people's souls. It is a negativistic religion. It is unreal. It unfits its fol-

lowers for healthy, happy living. And I would say the same
of Confucianism and—"

"But I thought Confucianism was a most practical religion."

"Not practical in the sense that Europe and the Western
world understand the word. Confucianism is a backward
ethics. Look at the bondage of the Chinese people for these
thousands of years. Do you think that their religion has
nothing to do with their condition? Confucianism is partly
responsible, a great deal responsible, for their piteous situation—their poverty, their unhealthy slums, their opium, their
unsanitation, their lifeless existence."

"And Hinduism?"

"I have no use for it either."

"But Mahatma Gandhi?"

"A failure and a fakir." He barked the words out.

"You remind me of Winston Churchill's estimate of him."

"Well, I don't mind being in the company of Churchill.
For he is a first-rate man—a great Westerner," he said, "active, dynamic, and with a stout impregnable heart. He is a
good representative of our civilization!"

And for a moment he continued to laud the ways of the
Western world as opposed to the east—the one with its admirable genius for organization and power, the other with
its inertia and dullness—and finally back to Gandhi again.

I began to understand Claudel a little better now. He spoke
very dogmatically and strongly, and I realized what a good
solid orthodox Catholic and Thomist he was. But it was de-
lightful to meet a man who spoke his mind openly from such
a vantage point of experience.

"I can't agree with you about Mahatma Gandhi," I said
stoutly. "I have felt that he is one of the greatest men of all
time—with his practicality in terms of the spirit, his religious
affirmation of the dynamics of soul-force—no, I don't know

any man of modern times who has excited me so much with his vision of man cooperative, man brother-to-brother, and man as a moral idealist winning victory over barbarity by the opposite of barbarity—character and peaceful perseverance.

"You are quite eloquent about Mr. Gandhi," he said with a little satiric smile.

"Yes, I guess I am," I said.

And then he went on. "Perhaps I am more practical-minded—that is technologically-minded—than you are. I do not like Gandhi's teachings because he seems to me to go counter to the course of history and progress of the human race. He cared nothing for art, nothing for beauty. He disliked machinery and the whole world of modern mechanics. How can you admire a man as blind as that?"

"But behind that was something else," I said, "some sort of idealistic enthusiasm and devotion which approached the divine—the divine in man as I consider it to be."

"Perhaps I ought to qualify my opinion about Buddhism," he said. "When I spoke a moment ago I had Indian Buddhism in mind. But Japanese Buddhism I rather like. And you notice that the Japanese have of all the Oriental nations marched along in the progress of the Western world. There is some sort of life-giving power in the religion of the Japanese. Perhaps it might be the other way round. Maybe the Japanese people have a vitality of their own and that vitality passes into their religion—from them rather than from their religion back into them. And as for India—though you may like Mr. Gandhi you will not like his country."

"Why not?"

"Well, I was just telling you what I thought of Asia as contrasted with Europe and the United States. India *is* Asia —the most backward country on earth." He chuckled harshly. "You good-hearted Americans give them wheat.

You create quite a pother in your press as to the right and wrong of the matter, and then, of course, in your charitable feelings, you rush over food for the Indians. Well, I can tell you what will happen to a great deal of that wheat. It will be fed to the useless sacred cows and to the sacred monkeys. You might remember that India has some—I am guessing here somewhat—has perhaps a hundred million cows. And most of them don't give any milk at all. They are set aside sacrosanct, and they must be fed no matter how hungry those who feed them may become. And then there are those monkeys! And the people worship the cobra too—worship snakes. And there are thousands of religious sects quarreling with one another. The children die in the streets. The country has been torn apart. A piece plucked out of its Eastern side to create East Pakistan, and a great chunk cut off from the Western side. And remember the recent massacres of Moslem by Hindu and Hindu by Moslem—each hacking and dismembering the body of the other. The other day I was reading a book where the author said that all religions are good. He was a fool. I will simply say he didn't know India."

"But what about Nehru, Mr. Claudel?"

"Well, no doubt Nehru is trying to do the best he can. He certainly is an improvement on Gandhi. He has respect for modern machinery and modern sanitation, progress—the whole new world of medicine and of chemistry and physics. Yes, Nehru is a great improvement on Brother Gandhi. Go and read Katherine Mayo's book, *Mother India*. It is perfectly true."

"I remember that Mr. Gandhi declared the book was false from beginning to end."

"Well, you wouldn't expect anything else from him, would you?"

Then he was off again crying up the virtues of the Western

world over the East. Finally we got switched around to
literature. I wanted to hear him talk about Russia and Russian
writing and politics. So I asked him what he thought of
Tolstoi.

"I don't like Tolstoi," he said. "He got loaded down with
a sense of being a great man. Maybe I don't like great men
—not such great men as he. He was a sceptic, unbeliever, a
sick man—he was scrambling around for peace, his own
inner life was always in disorder. He wrote vividly, but there
was no central nucleus, no point of view from which he could
speak. He was tossed about by all the winds of passion and
uncertainties and idealogics. No, I don't care for Tolstoi."

"And Dostoevsky? I remember somewhere in relation to
him you speak of le mélange broyé, the beaten mixture of
body and soul," I said.

"Yes, a man of anguish," he said—"but a great man—he felt
the importance of the church—his church, but still the
church. He was a man in the travail of the human spirit—yes
a religious man, and at times driven somewhat mad by pain.
A great man. Even Gide wrote a fine book about him."

"Even Gide?" I said.

"Even Gide," he said, and his face was unsmiling. And he
hurried on. "But as for your American writing—you have a
wonderful man, Walt Whitman. There was a singer. He had
hope, he had faith, and for that matter, charity. He believed
in efficiency too. I like him."

"I remember Gide liked him too," I said.

"But in the wrong way." And his voice was snapping
again. "And as for the writing going on in France at the
present time. True there is a great deal of decadence about
it. I needn't mention names. Yes, my poor country is not only
having difficulties politically, but it is also having them spiritually and aesthetically."

"Yes, in your correspondence with Gide you speak a lot about that," I said.

"You've read that? Well, you realize my point of view. This great man, Gide, was a very sick man too."

"I remember you described him as a cursed and unhappy being."

"Yes, a sick and cursed and unhappy man—*un empoisonneur*, a poisoner. Yes, how hard it is to remember *si le grain ne meurt*—"

And he hurried on into talk about American political leaders and politics. "Yes, I thought Woodrow Wilson was a great man—he had the right idea. He was not the most practical of people, but he had an admirable mind and an admirable sincerity. Yes, I have had admiration for Franklin Roosevelt. He got things done. He moved right ahead. Yes, a very energetic and wonderful man." He smiled. "You can see that I like people who get things done. I like people who love to work, who love to do, to accomplish. I hate lazy people. That partly explains my dislike of the superstition and fatalistic religion of the Orient. They don't do enough over there. They're too lazy.

"The League of Nations was a step in the right direction under Mr. Wilson but your country was too ignorant, was not ready for it—yes, the United States had a responsibility —has a great responsibility for what has happened in the modern world. We made many blunders here in France, but I think the most tragic blunders were made in your country. We suffered most in our country, but we have had least responsibility for the present tragedy."

And then I said that since he liked the political leaders who got things done then perhaps he would give me his opinion of Stalin who certainly had a record for that.

Mr. Claudel's eyes flashed. "I don't mean that because a

man gets things done he is necessarily a great man," he said, "or that they are necessarily the right things to be done. Our Bluebeard here in France got things done, yes indeed. As for Stalin, I hate him. After all, who can like Stalin, who can like oppression, who can like tyranny? Certainly you wouldn't expect a Frenchman to. But at the same time I must give thanks to Mr. Stalin, for because of him and his Russians it looks as if the United States of Europe will ultimately become a fact. The European nations are being brought closer together because of the threat of Russia. No, I don't have any fear of Russia. I am as sure as I am living that the Russian regime with its oppression and its restriction on freedom, with its police power, its autocratic and evil tyranny, will surely collapse. It is all contrary to the human spirit, contrary to what I believe in, to all the teachings of the great books and the sages and thinkers and people who have done mighty things in the past. I verily believe that all things that are not founded on truth must collapse. Only truth can sustain the fabric of man's building. Read the Bible. It is all in the Bible. Take the illustration of Mussolini. I prophesied his downfall —he was going contrary to the deeper righteousness of the world. And so he had to pass from the scene. I don't necessarily mean that I am a follower of St. Paul only. No, I also believe in the Greek genius and in the Greek philosophers and tragedians. I love their drama, their poetry. They marched in singing rhythms in the direction that man as a humanistic creature, as one above the animals, as lord of his universe has to go—marched along the highway which man should and must travel in if he is to fulfill the destiny meant for him."

"I have read your translation of *Agamemnon*."

"Yes, I love Aeschylus. I can never get enough of that great man. He had a religious vision, a truly religious vision of the universe. There was a sense of the spirit of the creator in him, of his own Zeus. The best edition of that translation is the *Mercure de France*. It is included in my theatrical works. You'll find it in the fourth volume."

"Yes sir, I have read it. And I also have bought the four volumes and brought them along for you to autograph if you will kindly do so."

"I shall be pleased," he said. "But we were speaking about Stalinism, about Russia. Yes, I do give thanks for this tyranny even so, because I think, as I say, that by means of it, Europe will be unified, and in such a union of strength France will move on to a great future, and the other nations allied with her will also move. I cannot reiterate too strongly that if we in Europe and you in the United States—including the British Commonwealth—if we stand firm, all the threats of Russia and any other threats whatsoever will fail. There is much, much work to be done.

"One of the first things that should be done is for your country to begin a close and deep study of other nations. Your country is in the fortunate position of being a leading world power—and I mean just that, a power. But I fear that your knowledge and your ideals are not sufficient to accompany that power safely, are not sufficient to guide you. As you know I am a great believer in the Bible. To me it is *The Book*. (He pronounced it 'Beeble.') From it we can draw lessons and teachings which will help us not only individually, but nationally and universally also. We need more religious instruction in our educational institutions. We need more acquaintance with the deep ethical principles of philosophy, and we need to absorb, to bathe ourselves, to splash about in the fine music, sculpture, painting and the various arts which man has given birth to out of his long travail, his hope and his endeavor. Nations must exchange their basic patterns of civilization one with the other.

"For instance, I think your own State Department men

are woefully lacking in training. I would like to see a training center set up, say in Paris, by your government. And here your young diplomats-to-be, your emissaries and ambassadors—the young men, could be sent for training. Let them learn the languages of Europe, let them immerse themselves in its culture.

"As I say, your country has great power, the question is whether she has the knowledge, the wisdom, the understanding to go with that power. The time grows short, and there should be no delay in hurrying along this endeavor."

"What do you mean by the time growing short, Mr. Claudel?"

He shook his head. "I mean vast forces and powers are being unleashed in the world—your atom bomb, for instance, the new possibility of germ warfare, the incredible adventures in speed—in short, the huge strides in methods and means of manipulating and handling physical actualities, materials, making them behave, making them do things, and doing them in an aggrandized manner, just as a little sprocket can build up a greater sprocket and a greater sprocket still —in a sort of multiplying progression. Man the engineer is in dire need of man the thinker, man the priest."

"Yes, yes, I agree."

"I am rather an old hand in this sort of political experience. You may remember I was a sort of midwife for the Kellogg-Briand Pact, and I often in these days think of the League of Nations and how your country wrecked it. But then, as the Bible says, first the leaf and then the bud and then the full grain in the leaf. Perhaps we will have to go through three stages. First the League of Nations, second the turmoiling United Nations, and third—I don't know what.

"But," he continued with great energy, "I have hope for the future. I even do not fear a war out of the present crisis. But men must work hard, and men must believe in the truth.

We in this country have made many mistakes, but now we are trying to remedy these mistakes. We must all give our devotion not to nationalistic loyalties and purposes alone but to something that is greater than these, to some truth beyond national boundaries. Men can unite in the truth, and as we search for the truth and for right action and for justice the more nearly and certainly we shall come to the united world, a world of peace and prosperity and of good hopes and opportunities.

"In your country you need a spokesman for democracy, for the basic principles and philosophies which underlie your government, which were spoken forth in such good terms, such glowing terms by Thomas Jefferson, James Madison and even your own George Washington. The world does not know enough about the United States, about its history and about its real beliefs. Too many people in Europe and Asia consider the United States to be crassly materialistic. When I was a young man I had that belief and I wrote many harsh things in which I spoke forth that belief. But the American people are a generous people, they are a kind people, and they are a cooperative people. But they also are emotional and not grounded in the course and tendencies of history. So I am simply repeating myself by saying that not only should America seek for wisdom but also it should propagandize the world as to the wisdom it already possesses and as to its own peaceful intent.

"The Bible says you must not hide your light under a bushel. I believe that America has a light and that it will not allow it to go out and that it will hold it aloft to help illumine the dark places of the world. That is my prayer." He fixed me with his eye. "I hope you pray." I shook my head. "Pity," he said, "you don't know what you miss. Yes. We all should pray for understanding at this hour.

"As I say, there is work to do. We cannot be slothful, we

cannot rest. Except as we work and produce, we shall perish. The Bible says again that a tree that does not produce good fruits shall be cut down and cast into the fire. I believe that the process of history is such that this works to be so and that a nation which does not produce good fruits will ultimately perish."

I hurried in a question.

"What do you think of the race question in the United States?"

"France has no racial antagonisms here at home," and he smiled and wouldn't comment further.

And then he took out his pen, reached for one of the books I held and autographed it. I shook hands and said goodbye. Out in the taxi I read what he had written—"Nobody hopes with better hope than when he hopes against hope."

A Sound Heart

Recently while in New Delhi, India, taking a look at the drama and music there, I had an interview with Sir Sarvepalli Radhakrishnan, the Indian Ambassador and Minister Plenipotentiary to Russia. I had met Dr. Radhakrishnan in Paris the preceding July when I was attending the UNESCO General Conference there and had talked with him a number of times and heard him talk about politics and literature and some of the present-day problems of the world. Also I had in times past read a great many of his books and philosophical treatises, including his big authoritative two-volume history of Indian philosophy.

When I came down to the ambassador's room in the Imperial Hotel, he was lying up in his little hard bed dictating to his secretary—his lap full of papers, letters and telegrams. But he had already said I was to come in whether he was busy or not.

I told him I had liked the speech he had delivered that afternoon at Parliament House on the occasion of the opening of the Philosophical Conference between East and West.

"That speech," he said with a grimace, "I didn't do very well."

"I thought it was good," I said. "Especially the last part."

He picked up a manuscript from the bed. "You mean the

part about the Greek and the barbarian, the Jew and the Gentile, the Christian and the Moslem?" he queried.

"Yes, and the Protestant and the Catholic, and the Allies and the Axis powers, and the Communists and the Non-Communists—and how we all must learn to live together in this world."

"Yes," he said, in his faultless English, "I suppose we all must stand by that sort of belief and work for it—all of us who hope for the safety and salvation of the world."

Then he autographed the speech he held in his hand and gave it to me. He also autographed a couple of books—his very fine "The Hindu View of Life" and "Eastern Religions and Western Thought."

And then the question of Kashmir came up. He shook his silvery head. "My country," he said, "has her problems. First the tragedy of the dividing of Moslem against Hindu, Pakistan from India. And now once more this mixture of politics and religion. There are four possible solutions to the Kashmir problem," he said, "and it is trite to say so. First, Kashmir can go with Pakistan. Second, she can go with India. Or third, she can divide herself, part going to one country and part going to another. Or fourth, she can vote to be an independent nation. Each solution is loaded with trouble and suffering. We must let time pass, we must pray for patience and forebearance. A tragedy, a tragedy!"

And then we got down to the matter of Russia. The Indian Ambassador knows that country as few people do, and I was anxious to hear him say something about our ideological differences with it.

And for the next hour or so he spoke out frankly and freely.

II

We must remember (he said) that we are faced with life and not theory. A fact is a fact. And no one can gainsay the fact that the Russian people today are better off than they ever have been. The welfare state is a going concern with them. But we must remember too that there is a lot of fear, suspicion and uncertainty among the people. They are ruled with a stern authority, but an authority intent upon their health and happiness. The people know it and so they accept their lot. They are not unhappy.

And the West must accept the situation.

As I said in my speech this afternoon before the Conference, the logic not only of life but of law warns us against either side's taking an adamant position. This is not conducive to peaceful settlements of antagonisms and never will be. In this Hegelian conflict some sort of compromise must be reached.

If we bring the truth, the facts, the actuality of life itself, the needs of the situation to bear upon our political differences, then we are more likely to reach some cooperative solution than not. Self-righteousness on either side is not righteousness at all. It is an evil.

If the West maintains that only its view is right, if Russia maintains that only her view is right, and each persists in that intent, then World War III and its horrors will probably come. And the light of liberty as well as the welfare of the people will perish to oblivion.

Can we not possibly take our cue from life? Life is a creative, growing thing. It changes, it moves on, it develops.

So let us remember that in the case of Russia, the people there, their life and their hopes—all are in motion.

Things go on.

What was true sometime ago so far as expediency is concerned may not be true today.

Take the case of divorce in Russia. We all remember that in the earlier days of the communistic regime divorces were easy to get. It was jokingly said even—that all one needed was to send a postcard. It seemed to many people outside the country then that the sanctity of the marriage bonds was being flaunted and even destroyed. Well, the Russians found that point of view and practice did not work. Today in Russia divorces are very hard to secure. So we see that even in a few years almost a reversal of policy has taken place.

Take another matter—that of co-education. Earlier in the regime, education was to be co-education. There was to be no discrimination and segregation of the sexes. Well, whether right or wrong, the Russian regime has finally decided against that policy. So now the practice is against co-education, especially in the lower grades. From the ages of seven to eighteen years the boys and girls attend separate schools.

And in the arts—music, literature and the drama—propaganda is giving way more and more to beauty, to self-expression itself. Everything does not have to preach the party line and that line alone.

I use these illustrations only to show that Russia herself is not an adamantine and unchanging tyranny or monstrosity of malpractice as so many outside countries maintain.

Therefore I am going about the world urging that we remember to devise and originate practices which take their touch and appreciation from the process of life itself.

Take another matter—that of the antagonism of the Russian regime to the church. Outside of Russia many of the free nations consider the Soviet Union to be the enemy of Christ, the anti-Christ, as it were, the demon fiend of atheism even. The truth is that though Russia was atheistic earlier in the Communistic rule, she has of recent years begun to recognize

that the church fills some sort of place in people's hearts. She
is realizing that man's hunger for the Infinite and for the
Unknown cannot be eradicated by fiat or decree. She is
realizing that religion is basic in the soul and fibre of human
beings, whether individually or communally.

It's true that members of the Communist party are still
forbidden to go to church or to have any traffic with the
church. It is still an atheistic party, believing that the church
fosters blindness, superstition and opiates (you remember the
old, old words) for the people's thinking. But after all the
Communists represent only a small percentage of the Russian
people. So the yearning of the people toward piety and their
humility before the mystery of life and the inspiration of the
soul is more and more allowed. In fact it cannot but be allowed. And so the church is playing a bigger part in the
regime than it did formerly.

Let us remember that. Russia too is having to change her
politics, her policy, her methods as expediency demands.

You ask me to say something or address some words to
your own country apropos of the now existing tension between Russia and—to use your own words—"the free
world." Well, I am very glad to do so. I for one believe the
heart of the American people is sound. I believe the American
people are a good people, a generous people, and they wish
to do the right thing. This I believe fervently.

But I also believe there are many wayward, ignorant and
prejudiced leaders in America who receive too much respect
and attention from your generous-hearted nation. I am speaking specifically of such men as your Senator McCarthy. You
will pardon me if I say I believe he is a poisonous influence.
I think he is doing great damage to the cause of international
peace—peace which all of us yearn for and without which
civilization with its arts will die.

You ask me also to suggest something as to policy. Well,

for one thing, I don't think that we will be able to settle these differences by mutual berating—beratings which continue to mount in violence in the forum of the United Nations.

I would suggest that America out of her great generosity must lean forward even more and extend even further the hand of friendship than she has before. But I don't mean to suggest for a moment that she should weaken herself, her power, her might. But I do think she could very well work out, create, establish and make apparent a better foreign policy than she has. It seems to me that her policy is too much determined by trying to pacify fears of Russia rather than being self-reliant, creative and inspiring in its own right.

You will forgive me for criticizing, but I know you are earnestly interested in these matters just as I am and as all right-thinking, good-willed people in the world are.

I trust you agree with me, as I said, that no people wish for war. We all want peace. But we must not be sentimental. Your country must not be sentimental. Neither should she be blind and prejudiced and confused by evil and ignorant beliefs and false fears.

Is it not possible for your country to work out a policy on a provisional basis of—well, barter? Let me illustrate. Russia is profoundly distressed by the possibility of the rearming of Western Germany. If, contrary to all promises and documents which have been stated and signed and sworn to, Western Germany is rearmed, then I prophesy to you, sir, that the world will have another Korean situation on its hands.

Look at that situation in Korea. Who has benefitted from it? What good has it done? It has been a terrible tragic dilemma, and the Korean people have been almost destroyed in the struggle between two contesting powers. It is not my business to say here and now just what the United Nations and the United States especially should have done or should do. I am merely pointing out that the Korean War is a tragedy and millions of piteous people have felt the full impact of it in their hearts. The liberators have brought the liberation of death, not life.

So if Western Germany is rearmed, I prophesy that Russia by means of East German soldiers will invade Western Germany. And we will once more have a war between brothers. And Russia of course will not fight. She will stand on the sidelines as before and she will grow stronger in the dilemma while the democracies bleed themselves to death.

So I say there is a chance that the German predicament may produce another Korean horror. Now why wouldn't it be possible for the United Nations—and of course I am referring very much to the power of the United States—why wouldn't it be possible for the United Nations to make a proposition to Russia? Let them say, we will do thus and so if you will do thus and so. As I say, this mutual bickering and berating and shouting at each other produces no results except worse feelings on both sides. So if a proposition something like this—I am not putting this down as the exact one to propose, but using it as an example—if it was proposed not to rearm Western Germany, to see that she remained as the conditions and terms of the surrender stated, provided Russia would withdraw from Eastern Germany, and then let the two parts of this divided country hold a plebiscite, get together under the auspices of say three or four neutral countries like Sweden, Norway, Denmark—or whomever would be chosen—then if a peaceful Germany could be united and made strong and set to healthful production again, this present terrible situation would be eased. I think it would be eased.

If this is not the right proposition to make, then make another one which would be—on the basis of we'll do this

if you'll do that—yes, work out one even which might re-
quire that Russia withdraw her power troops from the whole
of eastern Europe.

And also take a look at Japan. There again the future is
uncertain. If through mistrust and fear of Russia, the United
States rearms Japan, then what of the rest of Asia? The influence, the prestige of the United Nations is likely to die
so far as we in the Orient are concerned.

We do not want war. We are sick of war.

These great questions need statesmanship of the highest
order. As I say, the heart of your nation is sound. I think it is.
It can provide great leadership. But I must repeat again that
the evil counsellors among you are doing much damage—
much damage to us all.

III

At this moment we were interrupted by the entrance of
some visitors into the room.

"I'll be at the University of Oxford," Dr. Radhakrishman
said, "until March. You can address me there. And after that
I will be back at the Embassy in Moscow. Write to me."

He made his prayerful salute with his hands, and I went
out.

Asia and the American Dream

When I was a boy in school I often heard the phrase "The American Dream." Later on as I grew up I tried to get acquainted with the meaning of that phrase. And I think I did.

And now these long years afterward I still believe in it. Yes, believe in it more strongly than ever.

I declare there is such a thing as the American dream. I say *is* although there are many pessimists in our land today who feel like saying *was*. It still exists. But its brightness of late has faded. The dreamers don't dream as intensely and vividly as once they did in the days of Washington and Jefferson. Our last great dreamer in the American tradition was Woodrow Wilson with his vision of a world of free men united in common idealism and brotherhood. In some ways, Franklin Roosevelt, it seems, tried to follow after him.

And what is this American dream?

In his "The Epic of America" James Truslow Adams several years ago said, "We cannot become a great democracy by giving ourselves up as individuals to selfishness, physical comfort and cheap amusements. The very foundation of the American dream of a better and richer life for all is that all in varying degrees shall be capable of wanting to share in it. If we are to make the dream come true, we must all work together, no longer to build bigger, but to build

better. There is a time for quantity and a time for quality
. . . The statistics of size, population and wealth would mean
nothing to me unless I could still believe in the dream." So
said James Truslow Adams.

These are good words.

What is this American dream?

It is just that. It is a dream—a vision, an ideal of a nation
and of a world of other nations in which self-reliant men,
men of good will, of dedicated strength of mind and character live and have their being.

It is a theory and a commonsense philosophy of government which declares in its own ringing terms that each individual has his right of and his responsibility to the fullest
self-development of his talents as becomes the dignity and
worth of a man.

It is a dream then, an ideal of self-government, of liberty in
that government and responsibility co-equal with that liberty.

In short it is a religious dream. And its configuration and
essential statement were laid down long ago in Greek thought
and in the New Testament and in the teachings of a man
named Jesus Christ, who became our Lord.

It was also stated and written down half a millennium before
that by another great spirit and soul, Buddha, the Lord in
Asia.

And by Confucius in China and more lately by Mahatma
Gandhi in India.

It is a dream that has existed in the breasts of all good and
just-acting and right-thinking men of every age and condition and law.

Today the dream is being challenged, is being threatened,
and if it is to continue to flourish on this earth and grow
green with the hopes of free men everywhere of whatever
clime, period or condition, then each of us must become con-

scious of our need and our duty. We must get busy now as never before in the cause of well-doing and service to it.

For this a crisis of world tragedy and advancing horror is upon us all.

There must be no weakening, no yielding, no lying down before this monstrous barbarity which threatens us so direfully with its reach and ruin.

And what is this barbarity? It is hate and fear, and fear and hate.

The world is perishing for kindness.

II

I have just completed a trip of four months into several continents and many nations. And I have had the privilege once more of looking at my own homeland through the eyes of other people and of hearing her interpreted by alien critics on alien soil.

And neither by my own thought and words nor by the thought and words of others am I happy about my country.

Confusion and frustration are among us. And each day these vices would seem to increase, whipped into more frenzy and fervor by the very agencies which should seek to allay them and steady us in our moral purpose and solid intent.

The American dream as it was visioned forth by Washington, by Jefferson, by Abraham Lincoln and by Woodrow Wilson struck the heartstrings of the world in a great chord of harmony and friendship and admiration.

But these leaders are gone. Who has risen in their stead?

And daily we are losing more support and more friends in the wide world.

Not so long ago then the friendship of most of that world was ours. But today it is no longer true.

As Wendell Wilkie once said, there was a great reservoir

of friendship existing for us in Asiatic lands. Today it is sadly diminished and is growing less each succeeding day.

My main business in Asia and in Europe was to study the theatre, music and dance—those mighty and ancient forms of art there and to assist as best I could in helping toward the development of a living and effective drama which could play a constructive role in international relations.

But collaterally and out of the corner of my eye and in the small recesses of my ear as it were, I gathered something of the attitude of those many peoples toward us whether economically, politically or socially.

A young newspaper reporter in Singapore said to me at the opening of our interview—"What does America intend?"

I could not answer him.

That question is still being asked by millions of people in Asia and parts of Europe as they turn discouragedly toward other allies and another ideology.

They are confused by our confusion, frustrated by our frustration and infected with the fear which is our fear—a fear which strangely and viciously enough now has become a fear of us liberty-loving Americans.

For generations a majority of the Asiatic people have loved the kindhearted, the generous-souled American people. They have wanted to lean upon our leadership, to follow it, to work with us toward a united world and a better day for men everywhere. We have the physical power for such leadership, and until recently they have had the will and the urge to go with us.

But now in these latter days they feel that our ideals are falling behind our physical power. We are strong in the arm, but lacking righteousness in the heart and clarity of ideals in the head. The American dream is being betrayed.

So they feel.

Indeed they look upon our present foreign policy with

incredulity and dismay. They see us, the most powerful physical nation on earth, almost bankrupt and undone as to creative international thinking and dynamic policies for the healthful development of the world. They see a mighty nation run ragged by the Halloween ogre of Stalinism—a nation which in its hysteria identifies any and every kind of tyranny with communism and sees in every dark shadowy place of hill and dale some subversive agent or influence inimical to its safety and its soul.

They see a hundred and fifty million people burdened with a terrific taxation—of whose every dollar sixty cents goes to pile up atom bombs, aircraft, guns, tanks and create the galling harness of iron-footed war.

They see a giant with a great gun in his hand. And the heavier the gun, the greater the giant's fear. It would seem he has got himself locoed—ha'nted as it were, bogged in a neurosis of materialism.

So they think.

And Asia is becoming more suspicious and afraid of us than ever before. And we must remember there are more than a billion people in Asia.

In Malaya I saw it true. In Indonesia, in Thailand, in Burma and in India. And it has already for two years or more been true in China and Indo-China.

And what of Japan? That once mighty little nation has been brought low, been humbled, regenerated and set to ways of peace. She works and waits, unarmed and chastened, she works and waits. What will our policy be there? Shall we rearm her contrary to all treaty obligations and the very constitution of that country? Shall we, in our fear of Russia,— violate our vows and thus lose further the respect and friendship of the whole Eastern world?

And the same question applies to the arming of Western Germany.

III

We are losing friendships every day on other counts too. We are backing the wrong people in too many places. We are giving our strength in Asia and in Europe to effete and oppressive colonialisms, to authoritarian dictators and reactionaries—in Malaya, in Indo-China, in Formosa, in the Middle East and elsewhere. And all the while the people are crying for freedom, for bread and for a chance to develop their own lives.

And they are determined to have that chance.

The Minister of Education for an eastern country recently spoke their fervor and their faith when I heard him say— "Asia is on the march. She has waked up. Nothing will stop her in her progress toward a fuller life."

The Asiatic dream now is the dream that once we had and for which we fought our own revolution of freedom from tyranny. And it is a dream we must share in again, must make live more strongly again, or we shall fall further out of step with the march of the millions, be further isolated, and left finally alone in misery and second-rateness in our own graveyard of rusting military might. Our leadership will have passed to other hands.

This vision and ideal of a world of free and self-reliant men, of good men, of righteous men, depends on us all. It depends on you and me and upon how faithfully and devotedly we serve it now—here—today.

IV

And the American dream is after all no complicated or unattainable thing. There should be nothing confusing or frustrating about it. It is essentially a question of believing in right and wrong—the truth of right and wrong—and acting to the best of our ability in that belief.

What has happened to this ancient ethical code which inspired the conduct of our forefathers, which was the virtue of a generation only now growing gray? Our political leaders have forgot it. Rarely do we hear them say this or that is right or wrong any more. They pronounce on whether it is practical or impractical, diplomatic or undiplomatic, pro-Communist or anti-Communist.

And after all what is practicality?

In Asia I came upon a leader who still tries to settle problems, whether national or international, on the basis of what he conceives to be right and wrong. His name is Nehru. He is my man. He has my vote of confidence. For again and again and time without number he sounds his wise words in our direction. And we ignore them.

Prime Minister Nehru is trying hard to lead his country forward toward new health and life in terms of the new national order of one world unity! And he believes that unity must be based not only on technology, but on ethics—truth and right dealing. The two must go together.

And let us beware lest we lose his friendship, his guidance and the alliance of India—the strength and spiritual power of nearly four hundred million people.

Take the case of Kashmir. It is my earnest conviction that Nehru is seeking a settlement based on what he thinks is right—and what *is* right. I believe he considers it wrong that the United Nations under the domination of the United States might be hoping for air bases, military considerations there— if Pakistan should win the country—bases right next to the belly of Russia and in the flank of India's great friend, ancient China. In my opinion he believes such bases would increase the danger of the third world war and the possible destruction of India and her new ideals. He has declared openly that he thinks the continued manufacture of atom bombs is wrong, and he is willing to go hungry with his people to prove it.

Nehru is a man rare today in the world of diplomacy— a man of sterling character and unshakable religious principles.

Like Woodrow Wilson he has dedicated his soul to peace. He preaches peace. He works for peace. We need the friendship of this man. The world needs it.

Not only does the confusion and frustration of our international policy bring pain and anguish to the people of Asia, but many things about our domestic program fill them with the same dismay and apprehension.

I need only mention one—the race problem. There is no doubt of it, we are moving too slowly in alleviating this evil. We must speed our program up. The time grows short. We must will ourselves into more activity of justice and fair play. We must at the earliest possible time stop this penalizing a man in the privileges of citizenship and freedom because he happens to be more sunburned than those in power. It is a crazy thing to do, and the Communists are far ahead of us in justice and understanding there. And they are winning the dark-skinned Asiatics to their side.

They say that a man's soul has no color.

The recent dynamiting and killing of an innocent Negro citizen in one of our southern states reverberated about the world. And its reverberations in Asia helped to shake once more the peoples' confidence in our democracy. I know. I've been there. And I've seen the headlines in their papers announcing and denouncing this sort of thing. And even at this hour they are denouncing the lethargic legality which fails in most such cases to bring the guilty parties to justice.

We should not wonder that Asia shakes her head and says —"What does America intend?"

But I do not despair. As the ambassador from India to

Moscow told me some weeks ago in New Delhi—"I believe the heart of America is sound."

It is sound—and the American dream still lives in that heart. But it has become obscured, cankered and corroded over with careless living and too loose thinking. We must revivify it and make it live again. We must return to the principles of the dream—nay more, we must carry these principles still further forward. We must make them prevail more and more, both at home and in the world. For as we are morally strong as a nation, as we are on the side of right and truth—then the strength of our arm is a mighty strength. It is the strength of ten.

And these days of confusion and frustration will pass. We will make them pass. And the ethical principles, the simple principles of right and wrong, which energized George Washington, Thomas Jefferson and later Abraham Lincoln and more lately still Woodrow Wilson will shine again in their brightness and their glory in our hearts and deeds.

There is work to be done!

The Japanese Theatre

Last year I went on a trip around the world to study the theatre of a number of nations—among them Japan, the Philippines, Malaya, Thailand, Burma, India, Turkey, Greece and Spain.

Japan was my first big stop, and I have no doubt now it was the most important one.

From necessity I could allow myself only three weeks in that wonderful country. For soon I had to get back home to the business of making a living. Of course three weeks was too little time to learn much about the great cultural tradition and present practices of the Japanese theatre. I knew that before I started—no matter how much I read and prepared myself ahead.

But I had to compromise as best I could.

And I was kept busy.

Day and night I talked, saw, and re-saw and even dreamed Japanese drama and theatre. I looked at prints, paintings, drawings, pamphlets, posters, plays and actors. I went to the Noh theatre and saw for myself its famed asceticism and devotion to style and essence and comic interlude. I saw dance dramas and many gorging swollen Kabuki plays, both in Tokyo and Osaka.

I even sat through a whirlwind modern female revue in Osaka, and then in Kyoto City went to see the Geisha girls dance and play and hear them sing in dainty mimicry their coal miners' muscle-power song. I visited the famous puppet theatre of Bunraku in Osaka and watched in incredulity three full grown human beings laboring and sweating in servitude and service to each of those little lyric creatures of wood and wire and hair and cloth—the dolls. And one whole man was given over to working a single left arm, a job of ten years learning, I was told.

Also I went several times to dip into the great storehouse of native dramatic materials in the Tsubouchi Memorial Theatre Museum at Waseda University in Tokyo.

And I saw the stately court dances at the Imperial Palace. And out in the countryside I witnessed some of the more representative folk dances, and heard the people sing.

Soon after I arrived I saw the motion picture "Rashomon." I was enthralled. The man-woman relationship depicted in this film would have been the artistic despair of that imaginative misogynist August Strindberg. And other parts of it—except the ending—seemed to me to measure up to the best of anything on the present world screen.

But my concern in Japan was not with the motion pictures. They could take care of themselves along with radio and television.

The theatre!

II

Naturally first impressions whether of persons, art or things are not necessarily the true ones, and often they have to be revised even to contradiction when time and experience have yielded greater knowledge. But a reaction to any experience however brief is inevitable.

For the present then it is my belief that Japan has in the main the finest theatre art in the world. I have never anywhere seen anything to equal it. I say—in the main. And by that I mean that some of the elements of her theatre are the finest in the world. And these elements are in the production and the acting—not in the dramas themselves.

I refer to the Kabuki theatre and not to the Noh or puppet plays and productions. These latter may be fine too, but not for me. They seem too slow, too academic, too wasteful of manpower, methods and materials for an active, dynamic age.

But the Kabuki!—(The word, they tell me, in its three successive syllables means singing—dancing—acting.) And it is just that.

I have seen Kichiemon! Utaemon! We have no one in the West to compare with them. And I saw half a dozen others who in their acting go far beyond anybody I had met with in Europe, England or America.

The Kabuki theatre is the true representational theatre art as I've yearned to see it. It is the art which Appia, Meyerhold and Gordon Craig would have—even with their differing nature—joyed in. And they did.

What choreography! What color of costume and exquisite use of dance, pantomime and music! And the tremendous virtuosity and lyric reach of the acting!—these took me like the rich outpouring of a great glowing flower.

The nearest thing to this type of drama I had seen was the work of the Habima troupe and of Alexis Granowski's Jewish Academy Theatre in Berlin back in 1929. But in remembrance those seemed narrow, orthodox and message-slanted in comparison—however fine they might have been.

In the Kabuki theatre I found for the first time in my life all the elements, all the materials of stagecraft, organic and inorganic, completely seized upon and possessed by *mind*. Here was the full subservience of every recalcitrant principle to the vitalizing and leavening power of spirit. Here means became matter and matter completely lived in means. Style had transmuted itself into function and function became emotion and subjectivity of actor and stage environment alike. All had been given over to the God of Art—whole soul and body, as it says in the Negro song. In true Hegelian sense each existed and had its being in its other.

III

I will never forget the first Kabuki play I saw. It was eleven o'clock in the morning when I took my seat in the theatre. The slapping of the slats of the stage attendant had begun. They increased in tempo, and the curtain went up. A huge sigh of pleasure, of anticipation rose from the packed audience. The wide vast stage was bathed in a deluge of light. There before us stretched a fairyland of color, cherry trees, pagodas, an upland of pine trees, and in the distance the white mystic top of Mount Fuji. Seated across the foreground stage were a dozen stylized lords, followers of the Mikado, their wide rich robes billowing out and around them in waves of brocaded color. Motionless and Buddha-like they sat, and on a second level behind them sat another dozen of their fellows cross-legged, each in his own individualized and fabulous costume. The sharp plucking of the banjo-like samisens had begun, and the high lyric call of the narrator behind his windowed enclosure off at the left, starting the prologue comment and interpretation of the play.

The color of the scene filled the eye as an overpowering melody does the ear, and it was the more infused into the emotions because of the music and the words which poured out and mixed with it.

Under the impassioned intoning of the narrator's voice the different lords and warriors woke to life—the exaggerated make-up of their faces impassive and mask-like, each one bespeaking in his countenance the significance of grief, cruelty or anger as was the nature of his dramatic soul.

The story began, the action got under way. The gestures were large and slow, but emphatic. The actors began to speak, now in recitative, now in chant. The drift of the story was sensed. The conflict of wills and purposes inside the drama began to emerge.

Everything was pure intensity now, pure theatre, symbolized even and loaded with the "message" of the piece.

Suddenly there was a great clatter of sound on the narrow platform runway, the Hanamichi, at the rear, which led across the audience and onto the stage. The people turned, and there gleaming in the gear of war stood the villain, spotlighted and breathing out his red and smoking defiance. He thundered his way along the platform, stopping now and then in his motions of dare and do to build his pantomime to a climax—his whole advance to the stage a marvelous kind of dance.

The audience in the theatre sat there breathless.

And hour after hour they sat there so—while the play proceeded, music pounded, while the samisens gave forth their barbaric pluckings at the nerves, and the narrator's fervent voice rose and sank, sank and rose again.

The Kabuki theatre had them in thrall.

IV

But the Kabuki theatre is lacking the one final thing which would make it completely and all-round great—good playwrights with modern scripts. Its subject matter—whatever the fire of its production and acting—is like the Noh drama, too remote, obsolete, unimportant. It is too much taken up with dead ethics and empty loyalties—with puppet mikados, ancient shoguns, ronins, samurai, and the ever-present gutting sword of hari-kari, accompanied by the graceful foolish fan. Death, not life, is its downward pull and climax. The pageantry of the tomb is its delight and not the drive of the living present.

For this reason the modern young Japanese playwrights are opposed to Kabuki. Their eyes are now turned toward the West where "the land is bright." New ideas, new ways and means, must be brought in if the modern Japanese theatre is to flourish, they say. Kabuki must go, they declare. Down with Kabuki!

But if these young men in their mistaken zeal succeed in driving Kabuki out they will then in my opinion have destroyed the finest theatre existent today.

For here clearly to their very hand is the lyric theatre which so many of us yearning playwrights have dreamed about. Here is the theatre in which are to be interwoven in proper proportion the various elements of the imagination, music, dance, the impassioned word, all clothed in colorful costume and the habiliments of the poet's dream.

It is a matter mainly of proportion—of rightness. And certainly these young men have an opportunity here denied many less fortunate writers.

In the first place the modern Japanese playwrights have a fabulously rich national heritage of folk-lore, music and religion going back more than two thousand years to draw from—an accumulated honey-drip of human experience. And also they have the vital active challenge and opportunity of the present hour in the building of a new age for their country, the onward call toward freedom and spiritual greatness.

And they have in their Kabuki theatre the solution and the key for a new dramatic statement of all of this—of the nation's past, its present, and its future—a shining and inspiring statement. What more could any playwright want!

The Indian Theatre

They told me that one of the most famous actors and theatre producers in India was Sisir Kumar Bhaduri. And I was very glad to have the chance to meet and talk with him. A young Indian from the U.S.I.S. arranged an interview and picked me up at my hotel. He said he would act as interpreter if needed. And also he brought along a photographer.

We drove for miles and miles into the dingiest section of Calcutta and at last arrived at Mr. Bhaduri's quarters. He lived in a sort of broken-down apartment behind his dilapidated theatre. We were shown into a little bare room by an attendant and awaited the entrance of the actor and producer. Presently he came in—a very handsome elderly man with a fine broad face and resonant voice. He said he didn't want to be photographed with me or anybody else. He gestured us to seats, and then standing before us recited sonorously and dramatically a piece in his native tongue.

"A Bengali love poem," he said and bowed.

When he had received our compliments, he sat down and began to talk in fluent English.

"I understand you are traveling through Asia studying the theatre," he said.

"Yes, and music and dance too—as much as I can in a short time."

"What do you think of us—of our theatre art—Asia's I

mean?" His tone was suddenly bantering, and he cocked one of his heavy-lidded eyes at me.

"Wonderful—much of it is."

"And much of it not?"

"Well, yes, but that's to be expected," I replied.

"You've just come up from Burma, Mr. Basu tells me."

"Yes."

"That country is in bad shape, I hear. Between the English and the Japanese occupation, the people have been ground down, taken a terrible beating."

"But still they have their theatre going. I saw a number of good plays and some excellent folk-dancing too—in Rangoon and out in the countryside."

"I don't know much of what is going on there, but knowing Asia as I do—continental Asia—I would guess it's poor stuff. The Asiatics, my friend, don't care for art, any kind. They only love religion—religion and superstition. And Burma is part of the Asia I know. I hear that Rangoon is a dead city."

"It's been hurt all right," I said, "but a lot is going on there still. I met up with a live writing group—novelists, poets, musicians, and a few playwrights. Even the prime minister has written a play. I have a copy of it at my hotel."

"Any good?" and he peered sharply at me.

"It could be better. It's an anti-Communist piece, too much propaganda. But still I thought it was rather striking to find the leader of a country writing—"

"Hah, it will take more than writing plays to stop the Communists—either in Burma or in India," and he laughed mirthlessly. "And how did you find Siam—or Thailand as the new age people call it?"

"The people seem happy and well-fed, and their theatre is very active, very alive. No doubt the state subsidy helps. The present minister of education is interested in the drama.

In fact he gave me a play he himself had written—a non-political one, also one by his wife."

"Well, a state subsidy—uhm."

"I like the plays I saw, especially their masked-dramas. The use of music and dance was imaginative. And such pantomime! There is a drama school in Bangkok run by the state. Young girls and boys are trained for the theatre there from an early age. In this particular, Siam is ahead of any nation I've visited. Of course the plays still are pretty much aristocratic and old-fashioned, the subject matter still being drawn from their religious literature."

"Oh, yes, religion, religion!" he grunted. "And now you've come to look at us in India."

"Yes," I said, "and I appreciate this chance of meeting you and hearing you talk about the Indian theatre—if you'll be so kind."

"Sorry," he said, and he shook his massive head mournfully. "We've got no theatre in India worth the name."

"Oh, but you have. I've already seen a few fine things. I've met several young playwrights and directors, and there seems to be a lot of enthusiasm for—"

"Yes, seems, and only seems. The Bengali theatre which has been my love—the Indian theatre—is passing away. You know what is killing it—has already killed it?"

"No I don't, for I don't believe anything's killing it."

"If you stay here long you'll see."

"But I've got figures," I said, "on what's being done here. You have your eleven theatre organizations over the country, your Theatre Centre India, and then there is your people's theatre movement I've heard a lot about—out in the villages and rural sections—your traveling players and—"

"Pooh, pooh," he interrupted scoffingly. "Somebody's been filling you with—well, hot air. Talk, nothing but talk—and names, labels, and a few small pitiful amateur efforts.

Yes, the biggest and most important thing about these so-called organizations is their name. They give themselves a high-sounding title, and that's all. They accomplish nothing." He held up his hand to keep me from sticking in an objection and went on. "No, there is no longer any Indian theatre. I asked you what was killing it. I'll tell you—the motion pictures. Anybody that has the price of a ticket goes to see a wretched motion picture."

"Well, I understand there are a lot of movies being made in India—more than any other country in the world except the United States. But still—"

"There, you see," and he shot out his open palms with a fierce shoveling motion. "The movies! Long, long ago it was different. But now look at it. Look at me. For thirty years I have been on the stage—you know, thirty years. I was once a college professor. I gave up teaching for the stage. And for the last twenty years of that time I have not had a decent home in which to show my ability in my native land. I have had to move six or seven times lately from theatre to worse theatre. At this moment now the landlord is trying to expel me from these premises."

And he gestured around him with an angry and fervid hand, indicating through the window on a sort of corridor back porch a lot of household furnishings, desks, cupboards, and chairs piled up awaiting the moving van.

"If the state would only help us," he went on. "If the government would only get interested in us. But the state will not. If people with money would only help us to keep the tradition of our noble theatre going—the ancient tradition—when great things were done and great minds were at work. But they won't. So here I sit without any help, unable to pursue my art in its full growth and strength. It is a sad situation, very sad indeed."

"But Mr. Bhaduri—"

He smiled and shook his great silvery head again and plunged on. "I remember there were bright spots in my dark past," he said. "Yes, I remember as if it were only yesterday, the beautiful visit I made to your country. I went there with my own troupe of players, twenty-five years ago I went, and I gave performances there in New York. You will find it all written about in the daily papers of that great city. Your people appreciated and they still appreciate the art of the theatre. But here in India—no. Now and then I am able to get together a company and put on some sort of show. There are a few other old actors scattered about the country who are trying to do the same. But it is all a poor and piteous spectacle. I am playing here this week and I hope you will be able to see me. But you won't see me at my best. My heart is old and sick. I am not able to pay my actors, not able to pay rent on a theatre. I am discouraged. This is a sad business—the theatre is dying, is dead in India."

"But look at your dance, and your wonderful dance-drama. Here is an art which seems to me almost as wonderful and profound in its technique and imagination as the Kabuki theatre in Japan," I said.

"Ah, the Kabuki," he said, and his hands went out again, this time in a flourishing tribute.

"But the Indian dance-drama is a fine thing too," I said. "Rarely have I ever seen such absorption, such intensity in performance as your dancers give."

"Yes, we have some good dancers," he said grudgingly, "but we are talking about the theatre—the Indian theatre."

"Well, surely the dance is an important element in that theatre, in any theatre, isn't it?"

"Well, it might be," he acknowledged.

"In my country the dance is just beginning to be felt as an element in our theatre production. You are far ahead of us there."

"Maybe so, maybe so," he said sharply. And he sat staring off before him, his face heavy and tired. For a while he sat silent. It seemed as if he had no interest in speaking further. I tried to encourage him.

"I wouldn't be surprised to see a new age come in the Indian drama yet," I said. "In fact, I think all these different groups I spoke of show—"

"What age?" he said sharply again.

"Well, the times seem auspicious—the political situation here in India now being what it is. The two hundred years of foreign control are ended. You are free. That ought to help."

"We once had an age of the theatre," he said. "There were Bhasa and Sudraka and then Kalidasa. You know of Kalidasa, of course?"

"I know his *Shakuntala*."

"You like it?"

"Wonderful."

"Kalidasa wrote many other wonderful plays," he said, his face lighting up. And then he was heavy and sad again. "But nobody cares to see them any more—not even *Shakuntala*."

"I understand it was that play," I said, "which awoke interest in Sanscrit literature in Europe. You remember Goethe had something to say about it. The prologue to his *Faust* was certainly inspired by the prologue to *Shakuntala*." I was floundering around. There seemed no use in talking against his heavy and morose attitude.

"Yes, yes, I have heard so. Then next to Kalidasa comes Bhavabhuti." But then he shrugged his thick shoulders forlornly. "That was all hundreds and hundreds of years ago."

I tried once more. "But India is now taking her place among the free nations of the world. She has a fine political leadership."

"Bah."

"At least I believe so. I see no reason why your country with all of its riches of inheritance should not have a new flowering of the arts and especially of drama. You have here to hand all the ingredients—music, dance, basic materials of legends, folklore, and now with your growing sense of nationalism—"

"A nationalism of snarling dogs," he spoke up swiftly and angrily. "One state against the other and Pakistan ready to stick a dagger in our side." He stood suddenly up as if stung by pain and frustration. "Ah, my friend," he said, and again he shook his terrific head, "perhaps you will live to see the times that are coming. Not I. And maybe I wouldn't want to see them. The nations are all chopping themselves up in little pieces—in this, this internationalism that's sweeping the world."

"Well, thank God for internationalism," I said.

"You are blind. Only pride of nation makes a people create. And for all you say, we have no pride in India. I am an old man now. I am sixty-four, and I haven't got much life left for me. So I will go on playing as best I can here in my old theatre until they run me out—playing the ancient plays, not this modern useless stuff, playing to a small audience of old tired people. I had hoped to spend my last days in some sort of comfort and appreciation by my fellowman. But I have such hope no longer."

He straightened himself, lifted back his head, raised his hands and with gleaming eyes began reciting from Omar Khayyam—

> " 'The worldly hope men set their hearts upon
>   Turns ashes—or it prospers, and anon
>   Like snow upon the desert's dusty face,
>   Lighting a little hour or two is gone.

> " 'For some we loved, the loveliest and the best
>   That from his vintage rolling time hath pressed.

> Have drunk their cup a round or two before,
> And one by one crept silently to rest.

> " 'Earth could not answer nor the seas that mourn
> In flowing purple, of their Lord forlorn—' "

He stopped, pulled out a snow-white handkerchief, wiped his eyes and blew his nose a mighty blast. As the words rolled out from him I felt the hair tickling on the back of my neck and a cold chill spreading down my spine. What a voice! What an actor!

"Yes, as the poet says." And he went on wearily, the tears oozing out of his expressive eyes—

> " 'Indeed the idols I have loved so long
> Have done my credit in this world much wrong.
> Have drowned my glory in a shallow cup
> And sold my reputation for a song.'

"Sixty-four," he said stiffly. "I am old."

"But that's not old, Mr. Bhaduri," I said. "In my country it's not. And you're—"

"In my country that is a very old age," he muttered. "We don't live long in this country of mine, you know. Too much sickness, too much poverty, too much ignorance. No, we don't live long here."

And turning suddenly he stuck out his hand in abrupt farewell.